Swarm Intelligence - Recent Advances, New Perspectives and Applications

Edited by Javier Del Ser, Esther Villar and Eneko Osaba

Published in London, United Kingdom

IntechOpen

Supporting open minds since 2005

Swarm Intelligence - Recent Advances, New Perspectives and Applications
http://dx.doi.org/10.5772/intechopen.77539
Edited by Javier Del Ser, Esther Villar and Eneko Osaba

Part of IntechOpen Book Series: Artificial Intelligence, Volume 2
Book Series Editor: Marco Antonio Aceves-Fernandez

Contributors
Hiroshi Sho, Celal Ozturk, Sibel Arslan, Victor Coppo Leite, Bruno Seixas Gomes de Almeida, Francis Oloo, Huey-Yang Horng, Javier Del Ser, Eneko Osaba, Esther Villar

First published in London, United Kingdom, 2019 by IntechOpen
IntechOpen is the global imprint of INTECHOPEN LIMITED, registered in England and Wales, registration number: 11086078, 7th floor, 10 Lower Thames Street, London, EC3R 6AF, United Kingdom
Printed in Croatia

British Library Cataloguing-in-Publication Data
A catalogue record for this book is available from the British Library

Additional hard and PDF copies can be obtained from orders@intechopen.com

Swarm Intelligence - Recent Advances, New Perspectives and Applications
Edited by Javier Del Ser, Esther Villar and Eneko Osaba
p. cm.
Print ISBN 978-1-78984-536-5
Online ISBN 978-1-78984-537-2
eBook (PDF) ISBN 978-1-83968-000-7
ISSN 2633-1403

For EU product safety concerns:
IN TECH d.o.o., Prolaz Marije Krucifikse Kozulić 3, 51000 Rijeka, Croatia, info@intechopen.com or visit our website at intechopen.com.

IntechOpen Book Series

Artificial Intelligence

Volume 2

Prof. Dr. Javier Del Ser received his first PhD in Telecommunication Engineering from the University of Navarra, Spain, and his second PhD in Computational Intelligence from the University of Alcala, Spain. Currently he is a Research Professor in Artificial Intelligence and the leading scientist of the OPTIMA (Optimization, Modeling and Analytics) research area at TECNALIA RESEARCH & INNOVATION (www.tecnalia.com). He is also an adjunct professor at the University of the Basque Country (UPV/EHU), an invited research fellow at the Basque Center for Applied Mathematics (BCAM), and a senior AI advisor at the technological startup SHERPA.AI. He is also the coordinator of a Joint Research Lab. His research interests include the use of Artificial Intelligence methods for data mining and optimization. He has published more than 280 scientific articles, co-supervised 8 PhD theses (+ 9 ongoing), edited 6 books, co-authored 9 patents, and participated/led more than 40 research projects. He has also been involved in the organization of various national and international conferences. He is a senior member of the IEEE, and a recipient of the Bizkaia Talent prize for his research career.

Dr. Esther Villar holds a PhD in Information and Communication Technologies (2015) from the University of Alcalá (Spain). She achieved her Computer Scientist degree (2010) from the University of Deusto, and her MSc (2012) in Computer Languages and Systems from the UNED (National University of Distance Education). Her areas of interest and knowledge include Natural Language Processing (NLP), detection of impersonation in social networks, semantic web and machine learning. She has made several contributions at conferences and has published in various journals in those fields. Currently, she is working within the OPTIMA (Optimization Modeling & Analytics) business of Tecnalia's ICT Division as a data scientist in projects related to the prediction and optimization of management and industrial processes: resource planning, energy efficiency, etc.

Dr. Eneko Osaba works at TECNALIA as a researcher in the ICT/OPTIMA area. He obtained his Ph.D. degree on Artificial Intelligence in 2015 from the University of Deusto. He has participated in the proposal, development, and justification of more than 20 local and European research projects, and in the publication of more than 100 scientific papers (including more than 20 Q1). He has performed several fellowships at universities in the United Kingdom, Italy, and Malta. Eneko has served as the program committee member in more than 30 international conferences and participated in organizing activities in more than 7 international conferences. He is a member of the editorial board of the International Journal of Artificial Intelligence, Data in Brief and the Journal of Advanced Transportation, and guest editor in the journals Journal of Computational Science, Neurocomputing, Logic Journal of IGPL, Advances in Mechanical Engineering Journal, and the IEEE ITS Magazine.

Editors of Volume 2:
Javier Del Ser
TECNALIA Research & Innovation. 48160 Derio, Bizkaia.
University of the Basque Country (UPV/EHU), 48013, Bilbao, Bizkaia

Esther Villar
TECNALIA Research & Innovation. 48160 Derio, Bizkaia

Eneko Osaba
TECNALIA Research & Innovation. 48160 Derio, Bizkaia

Book Series Editor: Marco A. Aceves-Fernandez
Universidad Autonoma de Queretaro, Mexico

Scope of the Series

Artificial Intelligence (AI) is a rapidly developing multidisciplinary research area that aims to solve increasingly complex problems. In today´s highly integrated world, AI promises to become a robust and powerful mean for obtaining solutions to previously unsolvable problems. This book series is intended for researchers and students alike, as well as all those interested in this fascinating field and its applications, in particular in areas related to the topics on which it is focused.

Contents

Preface

Swarm Intelligence has emerged as one of the most studied artificial intelligence branches during the last decade, constituting today the fastest growing stream in the bio-inspired computation community. A clear trend can be deduced analyzing some of the most renowned scientific databases available, showing that the interest aroused by this branch has increased at a notable pace in the last years. Undoubtedly, the main influences behind the conception of this stream are the classical Ant Colony Optimization and Particle Swarm Optimization. These algorithms started the interest in this field, being the origin and main inspiration for subsequent research. Today, a myriad of novel methods has been proposed, considering many different inspirational sources, such as the behavioral patterns of animals such as bats, fireflies, bees, or cuckoos; social and political behaviors such as the imperialism or hierarchical societies; or physical processes such as optics systems, electromagnetic theory, or gravitational dynamics. This book focuses on the prominent theories and recent developments of Swarm Intelligence methods, and their application in all fields covered by engineering. This material unleashes a great opportunity for researchers, lecturers, and practitioners interested in Swarm Intelligence, optimization problems, and artificial intelligence.

Javier Del Ser
TECNALIA Research and Innovation,
Derio, Bizkaia

University of the Basque Country (UPV/EHU),
Bilbao, Bizkaia

Esther Villar and Eneko Osaba
TECNALIA Research and Innovation,
Derio, Bizkaia

Chapter 1

Introductory Chapter: Swarm Intelligence - Recent Advances, New Perspectives, and Applications

Eneko Osaba, Esther Villar and Javier Del Ser

1. Introduction

Swarm intelligence has emerged as one of the most studied artificial intelligence branches during the last decade, constituting today the most high-growing stream on bioinspired computation community [1]. A clear trend can be deduced by analyzing some of the most renowned scientific databases available, showing that the interest aroused by this branch has been in crescendo at a notable pace in the last years [2]. Undoubtedly, the main influences behind the conception of this stream are the extraordinarily famous particle swarm optimization (PSO, [3]) and ant colony optimization (ACO, [4]) algorithms. These meta-heuristic lighted the fuse of the success of this knowledge area, being the origin and principal inspiration of their subsequent research. Such remarkable success has led to the proposal of a myriad of novel methods, each one based on a different inspirational source such as the behavioral patterns of animals, social and political behaviors, or physical processes. The constant proposal of new methods showcases the capability and adaptability of this sort of solvers to reach a near-optimal performance over a wide range of high-demanding academic and real-world problems, being this fact one of the main advantages of swarm intelligence-based meta-heuristics.

2. Brief history of swarm intelligence

The consolidation of swarm intelligence paradigm came after years of hard and successful scientific work and as a result of the proposal of several groundbreaking and incremental studies, as well as the establishment of some cornerstone concepts in the community.

In this regard, two decisive milestones can be highlighted in swarm intelligence history. First of these breakthrough landmarks can be contextualized on horseback between the 1960s and 1970s. Back then, influential researchers such as Schwefel, Fogel, and Rechenberg revealed their first theoretical and practical works related to evolving strategies (ES) and evolutionary programming (EP) [5–7]. An additional innovative notion came to the fore some years later from John H. Holland's hand. This concept is the genetic algorithm (GA, [8]), which was born in 1975 sowing the seed of the knowledge field today known as bioinspired computation. All the three outlined streams (i.e., ES, EP, and GA) coexisted in a separated fashion until the

1990s, when they all erected as linchpin elements of the unified concept evolutionary computation.

The second milestone that definitely contributed to the birth of what currently is conceived as swarm intelligence is the conception of two highly influential and powerful methods. These concrete algorithms are the ACO, envisaged by Marco Dorigo in 1992 [9], and the PSO [10], proposed by Russell Eberhart and James Kennedy in 1995. Being more specific, the PSO was the method that definitely lit the fuse of the overwhelming success of swarm intelligence, being the main inspiration of a plethora of upcoming influential solvers. Therefore, since the proposal of PSO, algorithms inheriting its core concepts gained a great popularity in the related research society, lasting this acclaim until the present day [11–13]. For the modeling and design of these novel approaches, many inspirational sources have been considered, commonly categorized by (able to collect these sources in three recurring groups):

- Patterns found in nature: we can spotlight two different branches that tie (fall) together within this category. The first one is related to biological processes, such as the natural flow of the water (water cycle algorithm, [14]), chemotactic movement of bacteria (bacterial foraging optimization algorithm, [15]), pollination process of flowers (flower pollination algorithm, [16]), or geographical distribution of biological organisms (biogeography-based optimization, [17]). The second inspirational stimulus is the behavioral patterns of animals. This specific trend is quite outstanding in recent years, yielding a design based on creatures such as bats (bat algorithm, [18]), cuckoos (cuckoo search, [19]), bees (artificial bee colony, [20]), or fireflies (firefly algorithm, [21]).

- Political and social behaviors: several human conducts or political philosophies have also inspired the proposal of successful techniques. Regarding the former, we can find promising adaptations of political concepts such as anarchy (anarchic society optimization, [22]) or imperialism (imperialist competitive algorithm, [23]). With respect to the latter, social attitudes have been also served as inspiration for several methods such as the one coined as society and civilization [24], which emulates the mutual interactions of human and insect societies, or the hierarchical social meta-heuristic [25], which mimics the hierarchical social behavior observed in a great diversity of human organizations and structures.

- Physical processes: physical phenomena have also stimulated the design of new swarm intelligence algorithmic schemes, covering a broad spectrum of processes such as gravitational dynamics and kinematics (gravitational search algorithm, [26]), optic systems (ray optimization, [27]), or the electromagnetic theory (electromagnetism-like optimization, [28]). A recent survey published by Salcedo-Sanz [29] revolves around in this specific sort of methods.

In addition to the above-defined categories, many other fresh branches spring under a wide range of inspirations such as business tools (brainstorming optimization, [30]) or objects (grenade explosion method, [31]).

It is also worth mentioning that besides these monolithic approaches aforementioned, there is an additional trend which prevails at the core of the research activity: hybridization of algorithms. Since the dawn of evolutionary computation, many efforts have been devoted to the combination of diverse solvers and functionalities aiming at enhancing some capabilities or overcoming the disadvantages of well-established meta-heuristic schemes. Obviously, memetic algorithms (MAs), conceived by Moscato and Norman in the 1980s in [32, 33], beat this competition. Despite MAs were initially defined as hybridization of GAs and local search mechanisms, MAs rapidly evolved to a broader meaning. Related to SI, today is straightforward to find hybridization of SI meta-heuristic schemes with separated local improvement and individual learning mechanisms in the literature. Some examples of this research trend can be found in [34–38].

Finally, up to now, SI methods have been applied to a wide variety of interesting topics along the years. Being impossible to gather in this introductory chapter all the applications already addressed by SI paradigms, we refer the reader to some remarkable and highly valuable survey works specially devoted to outline the application of SI algorithms in specific domains. In [39] a survey dedicated to geophysical data inversion was published. In [11] the latest findings of portfolio optimization are studied. An additional interesting work can be found in [12] focused on summarizing the intensive work done related to the feature selection problem. Intelligent transportation systems are the crossroads of the works gathered in [40], while in [41] authors conducted a comprehensive review of SI metaheuristics for dynamic optimization problems. We acknowledge that the literature focused on all these aspects is immense, which leads us to refer the interested readers to the following significant and in-depth surveys [42–44].

3. Motivation behind the book edition

With reference to the scientific production, SI represents the most high-growing stream in today's related community, with more than 15,000 works published since the beginning of the twenty-first century. Analyzing the renowned Scopus® database, a clear upward trend can be deduced. Specifically, scientific production related to SI grows at a remarkable rate from nearly 400 papers in 2007 to more than 2000 in 2018. In fact, the interest in SI has been in crescendo at such a pace that the number of published scientific material regarding this field is greater than other classical streams such as evolutionary computation every year since 2012.

Thus, and taking advantage of the interest that this topic arises in the community, the edited book that this chapter is introducing gravitates on the prominent theories and recent developments of swarm intelligence methods and their application in all the fields covered by engineering. This material unleashes a great opportunity for researchers, lecturers, and practitioners interested in swarm intelligence, optimization problems, and artificial intelligence as a whole.

Author details

Eneko Osaba[1]*, Esther Villar[1] and Javier Del Ser[1,2]

1 TECNALIA Research and Innovation, Derio, Spain

2 University of the Basque Country (UPV/EHU), Bilbao, Spain

*Address all correspondence to: eneko.osaba@tecnalia.com

References

[1] Del Ser J, Osaba E, Molina D, Yang XS, Salcedo-Sanz S, Camacho D, et al. Bio-inspired computation: Where we stand and what's next. Swarm and Evolutionary Computation. 2019;**48**: 220-250

[2] Yang XS, Cui Z, Xiao R, Gandomi AH, Karamanoglu M. Swarm Intelligence and Bio-Inspired Computation: Theory and Applications. London: Newnes; 2013

[3] Kennedy J. Particle swarm optimization. In: Encyclopedia of Machine Learning. London: Springer; 2010. pp. 760-766

[4] Dorigo M, Di Caro G. Ant colony optimization: a new meta-heuristic. In: Proceedings of the 1999 congress on evolutionary computation-CEC99 (Cat. No. 99TH8406), Vol. 2. IEEE; 1999. pp. 1470-1477

[5] Fogel LJ, Owens AJ, Walsh MJ. Artificial Intelligence Through Simulated Evolution. New York: Wiley IEEE Press; 1998

[6] Schwefel HPP. Evolution and Optimum Seeking: The Sixth Generation. New York: John Wiley & Sons, Inc.; 1993

[7] Rechenberg I. Evolution Strategy: Optimization of Technical Systems by Means of Biological Evolution. Vol. 104. Stuttgart: Frommann-Holzboog; 1973. pp. 15-16

[8] Holland JH. Adaptation in Natural and Artificial Systems: An Introductory Analysis with Applications to Biology, Control, and Artificial Intelligence. Massachusetts: MIT press; 1992

[9] Dorigo M. Optimization, learning and natural algorithms [PhD thesis]. Milan, Italy: Politecnico di Milano; 1992

[10] Eberhart R, Kennedy J. A new optimizer using particle swarm theory. In: Proceedings of the Sixth International Symposium on Micro Machine and Human Science (MHS'95). IEEE; 1995. pp. 39-43

[11] Ertenlice O, Kalayci CB. A survey of swarm intelligence for portfolio optimization: Algorithms and applications. Swarm and Evolutionary Computation. 2018;**39**:36-52

[12] Brezočnik L, Fister I, Podgorelec V. Swarm intelligence algorithms for feature selection: A review. Applied Sciences. 2018;**8**(9):1521

[13] Gao K, Cao Z, Zhang L, Chen Z, Han Y, Pan Q. A review on swarm intelligence and evolutionary algorithms for solving flexible job shop scheduling problems. IEEE/CAA Journal of Automatica Sinica. 2019;**6**(4): 904-916

[14] Eskandar H, Sadollah A, Bahreininejad A, Hamdi M. Water cycle algorithm—A novel metaheuristic optimization method for solving constrained engineering optimization problems. Computers & Structures. 2012;**110**:151-166

[15] Passino KM. Biomimicry of bacterial foraging for distributed optimization and control. IEEE Control Systems. 2002;**22**(3):52-67

[16] Yang XS. Flower pollination algorithm for global optimization. In: International Conference on Unconventional Computing and Natural Computation. Springer; 2012. pp. 240-249

[17] Simon D. Biogeography-based optimization. IEEE Transactions on Evolutionary Computation. 2008;**12**(6): 702-713

[18] Yang XS. A new metaheuristic bat-inspired algorithm. In: Nature Inspired

Cooperative Strategies for Optimization (NICSO 2010). Springer; 2010. pp. 65-74

[19] Yang XS, Deb S. Cuckoo search via l'evy flights. In: World Congress on Nature & Biologically Inspired Computing. IEEE; 2009. pp. 210-214

[20] Karaboga D, Basturk B. A powerful and efficient algorithm for numerical function optimization: Artificial bee colony (ABC) algorithm. Journal of Global Optimization. 2007;**39**(3): 459-471

[21] Yang XS. Firefly algorithm, stochastic test functions and design optimisation. International Journal of Bio-Inspired Computation. 2010;**2**(2): 78-84

[22] Ahmadi-Javid A. Anarchic society optimization: A human-inspired method. In: IEEE Congress on Evolutionary Computation (CEC). IEEE; 2011. pp. 2586-2592

[23] Atashpaz-Gargari E, Lucas C. Imperialist competitive algorithm: An algorithm for optimization inspired by imperialistic competition. In: IEEE Congress on Evolutionary Computation (CEC). IEEE; 2007. pp. 4661-4667

[24] Ray T, Liew KM. Society and civilization: An optimization algorithm based on the simulation of social behavior. IEEE Transactions on Evolutionary Computation. 2003;**7**(4): 386-396

[25] Duarte A, Fernández F, Sánchez Á, Sanz A. A hierarchical social metaheuristic for the max-cut problem. In: European Conference on Evolutionary Computation in Combinatorial Optimization. Springer; 2004. pp. 84-94

[26] Rashedi E, Nezamabadi-Pour H, Saryazdi S. Gsa: A gravitational search algorithm. Information Sciences. 2009; **179**(13):2232-2248

[27] Kaveh A, Khayatazad M. A new meta-heuristic method: Ray optimization. Computers & Structures. 2012;**112**:283-294

[28] Birbil SI, Fang SC. An electromagnetism-like mechanism for global optimization. Journal of Global Optimization. 2003;**25**(3):263-282

[29] Salcedo-Sanz S. Modern meta-heuristics based on nonlinear physics processes: A review of models and design procedures. Physics Reports. 2016;**655**:1-70

[30] Shi Y. An optimization algorithm based on brainstorming process. In: Emerging Research on Swarm Intelligence and Algorithm Optimization. Pensilvania: IGI Global; 2015. pp. 1-35

[31] Ahrari A, Atai AA. Grenade explosion method—A novel tool for optimization of multimodal functions. Applied Soft Computing. 2010;**10**(4): 1132-1140

[32] Moscato P. On Evolution, Search, Optimization, Genetic Algorithms and Martial Arts: Towards Memetic Algorithms. Technical Report 826. Pasadena: California Institute of Technology; 1989

[33] Moscato P, Norman M. A Competitive and Cooperative Approach to Complex Combinatorial Search. In: Proceedings of the 20th Informatics and Operations Research Meeting. Citeseer; 1991. pp. 3-15

[34] Mortazavi A, Toğan V, Moloodpoor M. Solution of structural and mathematical optimization problems using a new hybrid swarm intelligence optimization algorithm. Advances in Engineering Software. 2019;**127**:106-123

[35] Osaba E, Ser JD, Panizo A, Camacho D, Galvez A, Iglesias A. Combining bioinspired meta-heuristics

and novelty search for community detection over evolving graph streams. In: Proceedings of the Genetic and Evolutionary Computation Conference Companion. ACM; 2019. pp. 1329-1335

[36] Govindan K, Jafarian A, Nourbakhsh V. Designing a sustainable supply chain network integrated with vehicle routing: A comparison of hybrid swarm intelligence metaheuristics. Computers & Operations Research. 2019;**110**:220-235

[37] Shareef SM, Rao RS. Optimal reactive power dispatch under unbalanced conditions using hybrid swarm intelligence. Computers and Electrical Engineering. 2018;**69**:183-193

[38] Osaba E, Del Ser J, Sadollah A, Bilbao MN, Camacho D. A discrete water cycle algorithm for solving the symmetric and asymmetric traveling salesman problem. Applied Soft Computing. 2018;**71**:277-290

[39] Yuan S, Wang S, Tian N. Swarm intelligence optimization and its application in geophysical data inversion. Applied Geophysics. 2009;**6**(2):166-174

[40] Del Ser J, Osaba E, Sanchez-Medina JJ, Fister I. Bioinspired computational intelligence and transportation systems: A long road ahead. IEEE Transactions on Intelligent Transportation Systems. 2019:1-30

[41] Mavrovouniotis M, Li C, Yang S. A survey of swarm intelligence for dynamic optimization: Algorithms and applications. Swarm and Evolutionary Computation. 2017;**33**:1-17

[42] Yang F, Wang P, Zhang Y, Zheng L, Lu J. Survey of swarm intelligence optimization algorithms. In: 2017 IEEE International Conference on Unmanned Systems (ICUS). IEEE; 2017. pp. 544-549

[43] Parpinelli RS, Lopes HS. New inspirations in swarm intelligence: A survey. International Journal of Bio-Inspired Computation. 2011;**3**(1):1-16

[44] Yang XS. Swarm intelligence based algorithms: A critical analysis. Evolutionary Intelligence. 2014;**7**(1): 17-28

Chapter 2

Use of Particle Multi-Swarm Optimization for Handling Tracking Problems

Hiroshi Sho

Abstract

As prior work, several multiple particle swarm optimizers with sensors, that is, MPSOS, MPSOIWS, MCPSOS, and HPSOS, were proposed for handling tracking problems. Due to more efficient handling of these problems, in this chapter we innovate the strategy of information sharing (IS) to these existing methods and propose four new search methods that are multiple particle swarm optimizers with sensors and information sharing (MPSOSIS), multiple particle swarm optimizers with inertia weight with sensors and information sharing (MPSOIWSIS), multiple canonical particle swarm optimizers with sensors and information sharing (MCPSOSIS), and hybrid particle swarm optimizers with sensors and information sharing (HPSOSIS). Based on the added strategy of information sharing, the search ability and performance of these methods are improved, and it is possible to track a moving target promptly. Therefore, the search framework of particle multi-swarm optimization (PMSO) is established. For investigating search ability and characteristics of the proposed methods, several computer experiments are carried out to handle the tracking problems of constant speed I type, variable speed II type, and variable speed III type, which are a set of benchmark tracking problems. Owing to analyze experimental results, we reveal the outstanding search performance and tracking ability of the proposed search methods.

Keywords: swarm intelligence, particle multi-swarm optimization, information sharing, sensor, tracking performance

1. Introduction

Generally, the task of tracking a moving target is an important subject as a real-world problem, for example, traffic management, mobile robot, safety guidance, image object recognition, industrial controls, etc. which are frequently taken up in various application fields [1–5]. In order to deal with dynamic optimization problems, many search methods are applied, and the approach of particle swarm optimization (PSO) in the area of swarm intelligence is one of them [6–11].

The technique of PSO is very easy to implement and extend. Based on its basic search mechanism, main advantages have three built-in features: (i) information exchange, (ii) intrinsic memory, and (iii) directional search, compared to other existing heuristic and evolutionary techniques such as genetic algorithms (GA), evolutionary programming (EP), evolution strategy (ES), and so on [12–15]. This is a reason why the technique of PSO is attracting attention and used in different fields such as science, engineering, technology, design, automation, communication, etc.

As is well-known, the search tasks handled by the technique of PSO are a mass of static optimization problems. The cause is simple for that the best information, that is, the best solution of swarm search and the best solution of each particle itself, is only recorded and renewed. Due to environmental change, the retained best information is not modified to normally search. Thus, its mechanism cannot adapt environment change or a moving target for dealing with tracking problems. Because of overcoming the disadvantage of the technique of PSO, and extending the range of its applications for dealing with dynamic optimization problems (including tracking problem), it is necessary to improve its search functions by adding some strategies into the mechanism of PSO [16, 17].

As prior work on handling the tracking problems by PSO, under a certain dynamic environment, we have proposed not only three single particle swarm optimizer with sensors, which are PSOS, PSOIWS, and CPSOS [18], but also four multiple particle multi-swarm optimizers with sensors which are MPSOS, MPSOIWS, MCPSOS, and HPSOS[1] [19]. And for confirming the search effectiveness of these proposed methods, several computer experiments were carried out to handle the tracking problems of constant speed I type, variable speed II type, and variable speed III type that belong to a set of benchmark problems.

In general, the search ability and performance of multiple particle swarms are better than single particle swarm for handling same tracking problem. The comparative experiments on the finding were verified in literature [20]. According to the obtained experimental results of the four multiple particle swarm optimizers with sensors, MPSOIWS and HPSOS are better in search ability. MCPSOS is better in convergence. MPSOS is better in the robustness with respect to variation in sensor setting parameters. And many know-hows on the useful knowledge such as their experimental findings are obtained [19]. As the search characters of particle multi-swarm optimization (PMSO[2]), however, the search information (i.e., best solution) obtained from each particle swarm is not shared to explore. For dealing with this issue, we proposed a special strategy called information sharing and introduced it to effectively solve static optimization problems [21].

In order to acquire further the search ability and performance of PMSO in dealing with dynamic optimization problems, we innovate the strategy of information sharing into the previous four multiple particle multi-swarm optimizers with sensors and firstly propose the four new search methods, that is, multiple particle swarm optimizers with sensors and information sharing (MPSOSIS), multiple particle swarm optimizers with inertia weight with sensors and information sharing (MPSOIWSIS), multiple canonical particle swarm optimizers with sensors and information sharing (MCPSOSIS), and hybrid particle swarm optimizers with sensors and information sharing (HPSOSIS[3]).

This is a novel approach for the technology development and evolution of PMSO itself. The crucial idea is to add the special confidence term into the updating rule of the particle's velocity by the best solution found out by particle multi-swarm search to enhance the intelligent level of whole particle multi-swarm and build a

---

[1]HPSOS has the search characteristics of PSOS, PSOIWS, and CPSOS, which is a mixed search method.

[2]PMSO, generally, is just a variant of PSO based on the use of multiple particle swarms (including subswarms) instead of a single particle swarm during a search process.

[3]HPSOSIS has the search characteristics of PSOSIS, PSOIWSIS, and CPSOSIS, which is a proposed method in PMSO.

new framework of PMSO [22]. Based on the improvement of the confidence terms, it is expected to acquire the maximization of potential search ability and performance of the four basic search methods of PMSO under the context of any adjunctive computation resource.

Due to the revelation of the outstanding search ability and performance of the proposed MPSOSIS, MPSOIWSIS, MCPSOSIS, and HPSOSIS, we take more detailed data from the computer experiments. Based on these obtained data, furthermore, we clarify the characteristics and search ability of the proposed methods by analysis and comparison. This is the major goal of this research.

The rest of this chapter is organized as follows: Section 2 briefly introduces three basic search methods of PSO and these methods with sensors. Section 3 describes the proposed four search methods of PMSO in detail. Section 4 implements several computer experiments and analyzes the obtained results for investigating the search ability and performance of these new search methods. Finally, the concluding remarks and future research appear in Section 5.

2. Basic search methods of PSO

In spite of the fact that there are a lot of search methods derived from the technique of PSO, they have evolved and developed from three basic search methods of PSO [23]. These search methods, that is, the particle swarm optimizer (the PSO) [24, 25], particle swarm optimizer with inertia weight (PSOIW) [26, 27], and canonical particle swarm optimizer (CPSO) [28, 29], are common ground for technology development of PSO and PMSO.

For the sake of convenience to the following specific description, let the search space be N-dimensional, $\Omega \in R^N$, the number of particles in a swarm be Z, the position of the ith particle be $\vec{x^i} = \left(x_1^i, x_2^i, \cdots, x_N^i\right)^T$, and its velocity be $\vec{v^i} = \left(v_1^i, v_2^i, \cdots, v_N^i\right)^T$, respectively.

2.1 Method of the PSO

The original particle swarm optimizer is firstly created by Kennedy and Eberhart in 1995. The method of a population-based stochastic optimization search is referred to as the PSO.

In beginning of the PSO search, the position and velocity of the ith particle are generated at random; then they are updated by the following formulation:

$$\vec{x}^i_{k+1} = \vec{x}^i_k + \vec{v}^i_{k+1} \tag{1}$$

$$\vec{v}^i_{k+1} = w_0 \vec{v}^i_k + w_1 \vec{r_1} \otimes \left(\vec{p}^i_k - \vec{x}^i_k\right) + w_2 \vec{r_2} \otimes \left(\vec{q_k} - \vec{x}^i_k\right) \tag{2}$$

where w_0 is an inertia weight, w_1 is a coefficient for individual confidence, and w_2 is a coefficient for swarm confidence. $\vec{r_1}$ and $\vec{r_2} \in {}^N$ are two random vectors in which each element is uniformly distributed over the range $[0, 1]$, and the symbol $\otimes$ is an element-wise operator for vector multiplication. $\vec{p}^i_k \left(= \arg\max_{j=1,\cdots,k} \left\{g\left(\vec{x}^i_j\right)\right\}\right.$, where $g(\cdot)$ is the criterion value of the ith particle at time-step k is the local best position of the ith particle until now, and $\vec{q_k}$ $\left(= \arg\max_{i=1,2,\cdots} \left\{g\left(\vec{p}_k{}^i\right)\right\}\right)$ is the global best position among the whole swarm.

In the PSO, $w_0 = 1.0$ and $w_1 = w_2 = 2.0$ are used. Since $w_0 = 1.0$, so the convergence of the PSO is not good in whole search process [30]. It has the characteristics of global search.

2.2 Method of PSOIW

For improving the convergence and search ability of the PSO, Shi and Eberhart modified the updating rule of the particle's velocity shown in Eq. (2) by constant reduction of the inertia weight over time-step as follows:

$$\vec{v}^{\,i}_{k+1} = w(k)\vec{v}^{\,i}_{k} + w_1\vec{r}_1 \otimes \left(\vec{p}^{\,i}_{k} - \vec{x}^{\,i}_{k}\right) + w_2\vec{r}_2 \otimes \left(\vec{q}_{k} - \vec{x}^{\,i}_{k}\right) \tag{3}$$

where $w(k)$ is a variable inertia weight which is linearly reduced from a starting value, w_s, to a terminal value, w_e, with the increment of time-step k given by

$$w(k) = w_s + \frac{w_e - w_s}{K} k \tag{4}$$

where K is the maximum number of time-step for PSOIW searching. In the original PSOIW, the boundary values are adopted to $w_s = 0.9$ and $w_e = 0.4$, respectively, and $w_1 = w_2 = 2.0$ are still used as the PSO.

Since the linear change of inertia weight from 0.9 to 0.4 in a search process, PSOIW has the characteristics of asymptotical/local search, and its convergence is so good in whole search process.

2.3 Method of CPSO

For the same purpose as the above described, Clerc and Kennedy modified the updating rule for the particle's velocity in Eq. (2) by a constant inertia weight over time-step as follows:

$$\vec{v}^{\,i}_{k+1} = \Phi\left(\vec{v}^{\,i}_{k} + w_1\vec{r}_1 \otimes \left(\vec{p}^{\,i}_{k} - \vec{x}^{\,i}_{k}\right) + w_2\vec{r}_2 \otimes \left(\vec{q}_{k} - \vec{x}^{\,i}_{k}\right)\right) \tag{5}$$

where Φ is an inertia weight corresponding to w_0. In the original CPSO, $\Phi = w_0 = 0.729$ and $w_1 = w_2 = 2.05$ are used.

It is clear that since the value of inertia weight, Φ, of CPSO is smaller than 1.0, the convergence of its search is guaranteed by compared with the PSO search [30, 31]. It has the characteristics of local search.

2.4 Basic search methods with sensors

We introduce the correspond to these foregoing search methods which are particle swarm optimizers with sensors to handle dynamic optimization problems. With adding sensors into the search methods of every particle swarm optimizer described in Sections 2.1–2.3, it is possible to sense environmental change and a moving target for improving the search ability and performance.

As an example, **Figure 1** shows the positional relationship between the best solution and sensors.

In a search process, the best solution of entire particle swarm is always set as the origin of the sensor setting. Based on the sensing information (i.e., the measuring position and its fitness value) of each sensor, we can observe the change of the

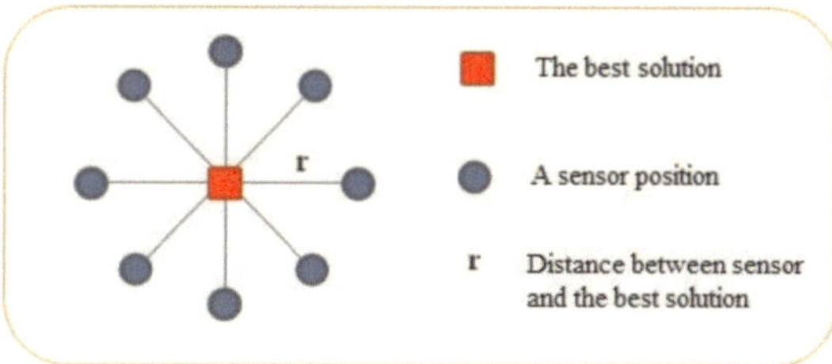

Figure 1.
Configuration of sensors.

surrounding environment and the moving target. In particular, updating the best solution by Eq. (6) is an important search information:

$$\vec{q}_k = \left\{ \vec{y}^{\,b}_k, \text{ if } g_t\left(\vec{y}^{\,b}_k\right) = \max_{j=1,2,\cdots} \left\{ g_t\left(\vec{y}^{\,j}_k\right) \right\} > g_t\left(\vec{q}_k\right); \vec{q}_k, \textit{ otherwise} \right. \tag{6}$$

where $\vec{y}^{\,j}_k$ is the jth sensor's position (i.e., solution) at time k, $\vec{y}^{\,b}_k$ is the best solution for sensor detection, and $g_t(\cdot)$ is the criterion for evaluation at time t.

On the other hand, regarding whether there are environmental change and a moving target or not, it is implemented by using the following judgment criterion:

$$\Delta_k = g_t\left(\vec{q}_{k-1}\right) - g_{t-1}\left(\vec{q}_{k-1}\right) < 0 \tag{7}$$

where Δ_k is the difference in the fitness values between different functions at the best solution $\vec{q}_{k-1}$.

If the judgment result of Eq. (7) is satisfied in a search process, the moving target has occurred. The particle swarm is initialized at the time and then continuous to begin particle swarm search. However, such initialization is not considered on the continuity of environmental change; it is implemented around the coordinate origin of the search range. As a new problem in the situation, if the distance before and after movement becomes smaller, the time loss to search is greater for finding out the new best solution.

By changing the coordinate origin of the initialization to the position of the best solution, the above difficulty can be dissolved. Therefore, the best solution of whole particle swarm is intermittently updated by sensing information.

And adding the judgment operation of Eqs. (6) and (7) into each method described in Sections 2.1–2.3, the constructions of the search methods, that is, particle swarm optimizer with sensors (PSOS), particle swarm optimizer with inertia weight with sensors (PSOIWS), and canonical particle swarm optimizer with sensors (CPSOS), can be conflated and completed to deal with the given tracking problems.

3. Basic search methods of PMSO

Formally, there are a lot of the methods about PMSO [32]. For understanding the formation and methodology of these proposed methods, let us assume that the multi-swarm consists of multiple single swarms. The corresponding three kinds of particle swarm optimizers described in Sections 2.1–2.3 can be generated by construction and parallel computation [33]. Therefore, these constructed particle multi-swarm optimizers, i.e. multiple particle swarm optimizers (MPSO), are multiple particle swarm optimizers with inertia weight (MPSOIW), multiple canonical particle swarm optimizers (MCPSO), and hybrid particle swarm optimizers (HPSO), respectively.

Based on the development of the search methods in Section 2.4, similarly, multiple particle swarm optimizers with sensors (MPSOS), multiple particle swarm optimizers with inertia weight with sensors (MPSOIWS), multiple canonical particle swarm optimizers with sensors (MCPSOS), and hybrid particle swarm optimizers with sensors (HPSOS) were acquired by programming [19].

However, all of their updating rules have two confidence terms in the Eqs. (2), (3), and (5) to be only used for calculating the particle's velocity. Because of the use of the mechanism to search, they are called as the elementary basic methods with sensors of PMSO which have the same updating rule of the particle's velocity [20, 34].

For improving the search ability and performance of the previous described elementary multiple particle swarm optimizers, furthermore, we add the special confidence term into the updating rule of the particle's velocity by the best solution found out by the multi-swarm search, respectively. According to this extended procedure, the four basic search methods of PMSO, that is, MPSOSIS, MPSOIWSIS, MCPSOSIS, and HPSOSIS, can be constructed [18]. Consequently, these basic search methods of PMSO augmented with the strategy of multi-swarm information sharing are proposed [22].

It is clear that the added confidence term perfectly is in accordance with the fundamental construction principle of PSO. And the effectiveness of the methods has been verified by our experimental results [21].

3.1 Method of MPSOSIS

On basis of the above description of PMSO, as the mechanism of the proposed MPSOSIS, the updating rule of each particle's velocity is defined as follows:

$$\vec{v}^{\,i}_{k+1} = w_0 \vec{v}^{\,i}_k + w_1 \vec{r}_1 \otimes \left(\vec{p}^{\,i}_k - \vec{x}^{\,i}_k\right) + w_2 \vec{r}_2 \otimes \left(\vec{q}_k - \vec{x}^{\,i}_k\right) + w_3 \vec{r}_3 \otimes \left(\vec{s}_k - \vec{x}^{\,i}_k\right) \tag{8}$$

where $\vec{s}_k$ $\left(= \arg\max_{j=1,\cdots,S} \left\{ g\left(\vec{q}_k\right)_j \right\}\right)$. S is the number of the used swarms and is the best solution chosen from the best solution of each swarm, w_3 is a new confidence coefficient for the multi-swarm, and $\vec{r}_3$ is a random vector in which each element is uniformly distributed over the range $[0, 1]$.

Since $w_0 = 1.0$ is used in each particle swarm search, the convergence of MPSOSIS is not better than the PSO.

3.2 Method of MPSOIWSIS

In same way as the mechanism of MPSOSIS, the updating rule of each particle's velocity of the proposed MPSOIWSIS is defined as follows:

$$\vec{v}^{\,i}_{k+1} = w(k) \vec{v}^{\,i}_k + w_1 \vec{r}_1 \otimes \left(\vec{p}^{\,i}_k - \vec{x}^{\,i}_k\right) + w_2 \vec{r}_2 \otimes \left(\vec{q}_k - \vec{x}^{\,i}_k\right) + w_3 \vec{r}_3 \otimes \left(\vec{s}_k - \vec{x}^{\,i}_k\right) \tag{9}$$

Since Eqs. (3) and (6) are alike in formulation, the description of the symbols in Eq. (9) is omitted. Similarly, the convergence of MPSOIWSIS is as same as that of PSOIW.

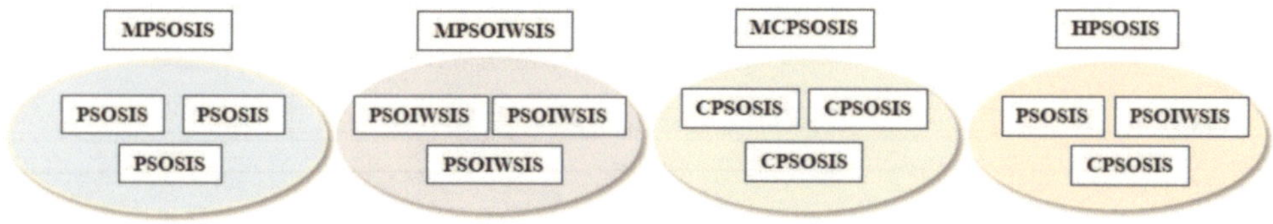

Figure 2.
The constitutional concept of the proposed four basic search methods with sensors of PMSO.

3.3 Method of MCPSOSIS

Similar to the mechanism of MPSOSIS, the updating rule of each particle's velocity of the proposed MCPSOSIS is defined as follows:

$$\vec{v}^{\,i}_{k+1} = \Phi\left(\vec{v}^{\,i}_{k} + w_1\vec{r_1} \otimes \left(\vec{p}^{\,i}_{k} - \vec{x}^{\,i}_{k}\right) + w_2\vec{r_2} \otimes \left(\vec{q_k} - \vec{x}^{\,i}_{k}\right) + w_3\vec{r_3} \otimes \left(\vec{s_k} - \vec{x}^{\,i}_{k}\right)\right) \tag{10}$$

Likewise, the description of the symbols in Eq. (10) is omitted. Since $\Phi = w_0 = 0.729$, the convergence of MCPSOSIS is as same as that of CPSO.

3.4 Method of HPSOSIS

Based on the three search methods described in Sections 3.1–3.3, there are the three updating rules of each particle's velocity in the proposed HPSOSIS. The mechanism of HPSOSIS is determined by Eqs. (8)–(10).

Due to the mixed effect and performance in whole search process, global search and asymptotical/local search are implemented simultaneously for dealing with a given optimization problem. It is obvious that HPSOSIS has all search characteristics of the three basic methods, that is, PSO, PSOIW, and CPSO. Similarly, the convergence of HPSOSIS is as same as that of HPSOS.

Based on the development of these methods in Section 2.4, here, we propose the four basic methods with sensors of PMSO and describe the search methods with sensors, that is, MPSOSIS, MPSOIWSIS, MCPSOSIS, and HPSOSIS, respectively, by constructing the particle swarm optimizers with sensors described in Sections 3.1–3.3.

For indicating the image relation of the above described methods with sensors, **Figure 2** simply shows the constitutional concept of the proposed four basic search methods with sensors of PMSO. It is clear that HPSOSIS is a mixed method which is composed of PSOSIS, PSOIWSIS, and CPSOSIS. Thus, HPSOSIS has different characteristics of the above methods as a special basic search method with sensors of PMSO [18].

Regarding the convergence of the above proposed methods, it can be said that the MPSOSIS has the characteristics of global search, MPSOIWSIS has the characteristics of asymptotical/local search, and MCPSOSIS has the characteristics of local search. With different search features, HPSOSIS has the characteristics of the above three search methods. In a search process, it is expected to improve the potential search ability and performance of PMSO without additional calculation resource.

4. Computer experiments and result analysis

Due to the track of a moving target, the setting parameters of each proposed method described in Section 2.1 are used in every search case. The main parameters are shown in **Table 1** for the following computer experiments.

Parameter	Value
Number of the used swarms, S	3
Number of particles in a swarm, Z	10
Total number of particle search, K	800
Radius of moving target, R	2.0
Number of sensors, m	5, 8, 11, 14
Sensing distance, r	0.0, 0.1, ⋯, 1.0

Table 1.
Major parameters for handling the given tracking problems in computer experiments.

The computing environment and software tool are given as follows:

- DELL: OPTIPLEX 3020, Intel(R) core (TM) i5-4590
- CPU: 3.30GHz; RAM: 8.0GB
- Mathematica: ver. 11.3

The tracking problems of constant speed I type, variable speed II type, and variable speed III type are used in the following computer experiments. A target object and its moving trajectories are shown in **Figure 3**. The search range of all cases is limited to $\Omega \in (-5.12, 5.12)^2$.

The criterion of the moving target is expressed as follows:

$$g_t\left(\vec{x}_k\right) = \frac{1}{1 + \left(x_k^1 - x_a(t)\right)^2 + \left(x_k^2 - x_b(t)\right)^2}\Bigg|_{t \in T} \tag{11}$$

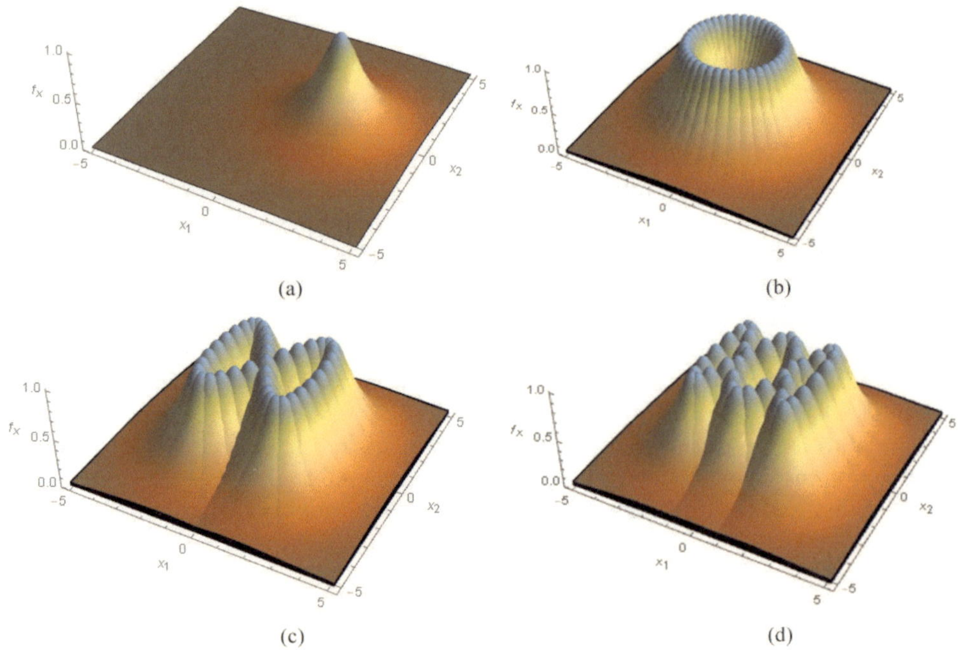

Figure 3.
Trajectories of the moving target. (a) Target object, (b) moving trajectory of constant speed I type, (c) moving trajectory of variable speed II type, and (d) moving trajectory of variable speed III type.

where $(x_a(t), x_b(t))$ is the center coordination (position) of the moving target at t time. T is a set of time series.

Specifically, for the moving trajectory of constant speed I type, $(x_a(t), x_b(t))$ is given as follows:

$$\begin{pmatrix} x_a(t) \\ x_b(t) \end{pmatrix} = R \times \begin{pmatrix} \cos\left(\frac{2\pi}{K} \times t\right) \\ \sin\left(\frac{2\pi}{K} \times t\right) \end{pmatrix}, \quad t \in T = \{0, 20, 40, \cdots, K\} \tag{12}$$

where K is the total number of searching on the whole circle of the particle swarm search. The target object goes 40 steps with a regular interval for the tracking problem of constant speed I type, the radius R of its trajectory is 2.0, and the fitness value of center (vertex) position of the moving target is 1.0.

The moving trajectories of variable speed II type and variable speed III type and their passing points, $(x_a(t), x_b(t))$, are determined by adjusting the coefficient of the time t up to two and three times for calculating $x_b(t)$, respectively.

The difficulty index (DI) for handling these tracking problems shown in **Figure 3(b)–(d)** is defined as follows:

$$DI = \frac{D_{max}}{D_{min}} \tag{13}$$

where D_{max} and $D_{min}(\neq 0)$ are the distance between maximum and minimum of the moving target object used, respectively.

By concreting calculation, the *DIs* of the tracking problems of constant speed I type, variable speed II type, and variable speed III type are 1.0, 3.06, and 5.39, respectively.

4.1 Characteristics of tracking target

In this section, we implement the proposed methods, that is, MPSOSIS, MPSOIWSIS, MCPSOSIS, and HPSOSIS, respectively, for handling the three tracking problems shown in **Figure 3** and investigating their search ability and performance in detail.

First, MPSOSIS, MPSOIWSIS, MCPSOSIS, and HPSOSIS were performed[4] to handle the tracking problem of constant speed I type which has a low-level of difficulty, respectively. As an example, the obtained change patterns of the fitness value of the best solution and the moving trajectory are shown in **Figure 4**.

We can see that the obtained variation of the best solution in whole search process from the left parts of **Figure 4** and the search trajectories are beautifully drawn from the right parts of **Figure 4(a)–(d)**, except for **Figure 4(a)**. And comparing to the left parts of **Figure 4(a)–(d)**, a big difference of the search state is clear with the origin of searching range as the center of initialization and the best solution as the center of initialization. The moving trajectories of the latter are relatively flat.

Moreover, when the target object moves, the fitness value of the best solution of the particle multi-swarm suddenly drops, then it rapidly rises with the subsequent search, and it is found that the peak of the target object is attained again. On the other hand, depending on the variation in the fitness value in the time space of

[4]The search time is about 1.3 s for handling the tracking problem of constant speed I type.

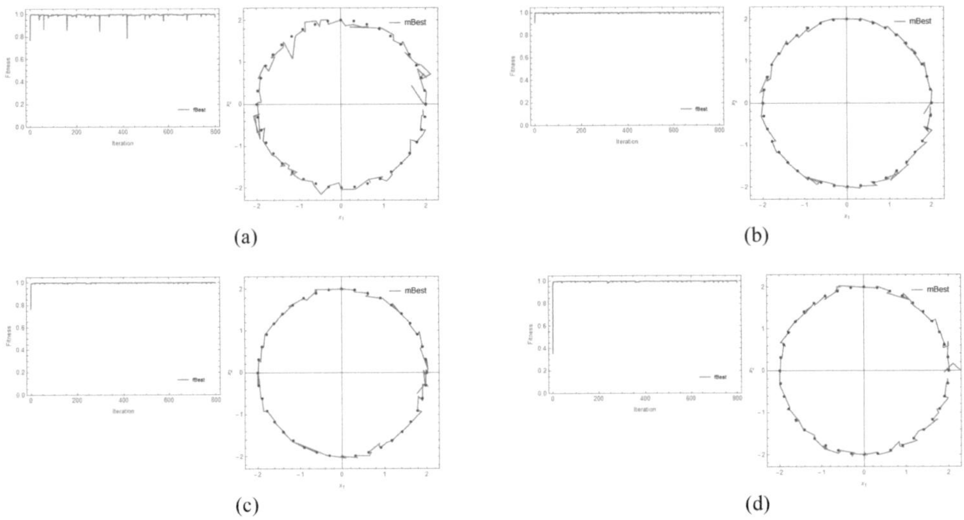

Figure 4.
The moving trajectory of the best solution for handling the tracking problem of constant speed I type. Left part, time space; right part, search space. (a) MPSOSIS case, (b) MPSOIWSIS case, (c) MCPSOSIS case, and (d) HPSOSIS case.

Figure 4, the obtained results show that MPSOIWSIS, MCPSOSIS, and HPSOSIS have good search ability and tracking performance depending on the variation patterns of the fitness values on the search space.

Next, for handling the tracking problem of variable speed II type which has a middle level of difficulty, MPSOSIS, MPSOIWSIS, MCPSOSIS, and HPSOSIS were performed, respectively. The obtained experimental results are shown in **Figure 5**.

We can see that the variation of the obtained best solution in whole search process from the left parts of **Figure 5(a)–(d)**, and the moving trajectories of

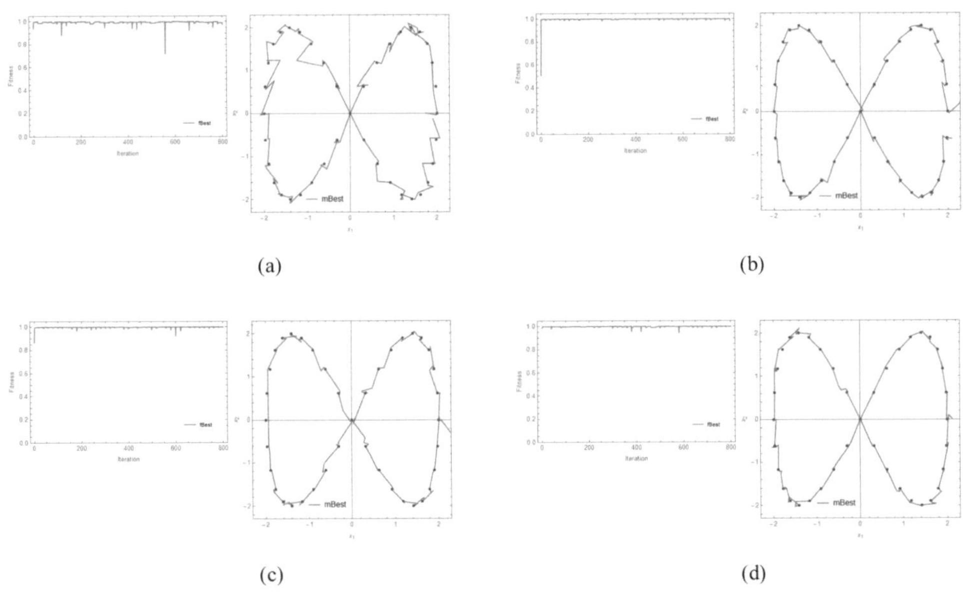

Figure 5.
The moving trajectory of the best solution for handling the tracking problem of variable speed II type. Left part, time space; right part, search space. (a) MPSOSIS case, (b) MPSOIWSIS case, (c) MCPSOSIS case, and (d) HPSOSIS case.

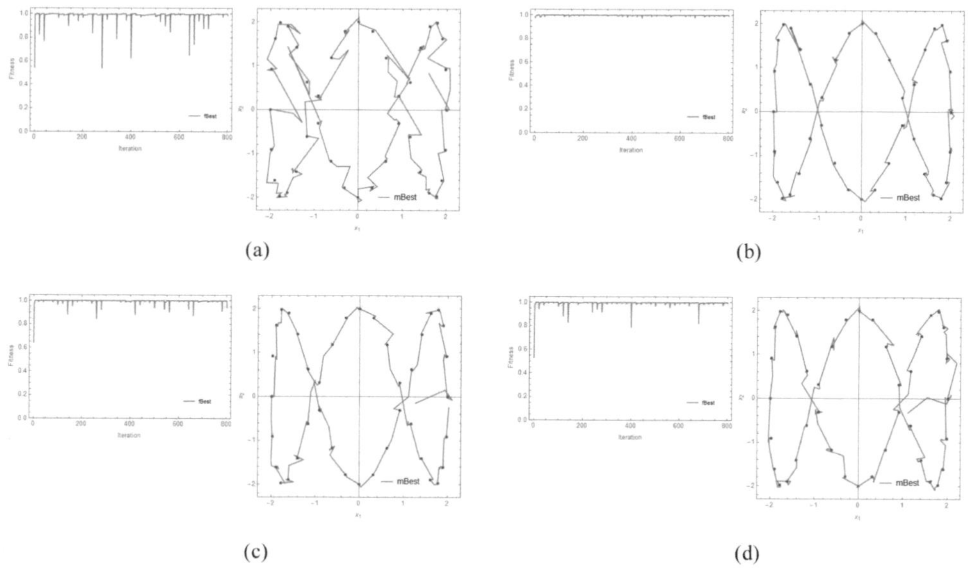

Figure 6.
The moving trajectory of the best solution for handling the tracking problem of variable speed III type. Left part, time space; right part, search space. (a) MPSOSIS case, (b) MPSOIWSIS case, (c) MCPSOSIS case, and (d) HPSOSIS case.

variable speed II type are drawn almost smoothly from the right parts of **Figure 5** except for **Figure 5(a)**. Then, compared to the variation in the fitness value in the time space of **Figure 5**, it is found that the falling range of the fitness value of the best solution is slightly bigger due to the increase in difficulty of the given search problem.

Subsequently, for handling the tracking problem of variable speed III type which has a high level of difficulty, MPSOSIS, MPSOIWSIS, MCPSOSIS, and HPSOSIS were performed, respectively. **Figure 6** shows the obtained experimental results.

Similarly, we can see that the variation of search patterns in the time space of **Figure 6(a)–(d)** for handling the given tracking problem. Except for the search result of **Figure 6(a)**, the search trajectories of **Figure 6(b)–(d)** are roughly drawn. Then, compared with the variation in the fitness value in the time space of **Figure 6**, it is found that the falling variation of the fitness value of the best solution is bigger due to the increase in the difficulty of the given tracking problem.

The moving trajectories of MPSOIWSIS, MCPSOSIS, and HPSOSIS are roughly drawn. Corresponding to this situation, it is clear that the smoothness of the moving trajectory gradually deteriorated as the difficulty level of the tracking problem increased. In addition, we can see that MPSOIWSIS, MCPSOSIS, and HPSOSIS are more susceptible to target variation compared with MPSOSIS.

4.2 Effect of the number and sensing distance of sensors

For objectively and quantitatively evaluating the tracking ability and performance of the proposed methods, we use an indicator such as cumulative fitness (CF) for estimating the moving trajectory of the best solution. The CF is defined as the following equation:

$$CF = \frac{1}{K} \sum_{t \in T,\, k=1}^{K} g_t\left(\vec{s_k}\right) \tag{14}$$

Consequently, by changing the number m of the used sensors and changing the sensing distance r, we implemented MPSOSIS, MPSOIWSIS, MCPSOSIS, and HPSOSIS to investigate their search ability and performance, respectively.

Hereinafter, we change the number m of the used sensors and the sensing distance r and implement the proposed methods for handling the given tracking problems.

First, computer experiments were carried out to handle the tracking problem of constant tracking I type. In this case, the obtained search results (average value of running ten times) are shown in **Figure 7**.

Comparing the search results of MPSOSIS, MPSOIWSIS, MCPSOSIS, and HPSOSIS shown in **Figure 7**, it is found that the difference in tracking performance regarding the existence of sensors is very large with regard to the search ability. That is, when $r = 0$, they become the search results of the existing methods, that is, MPSOIS, MPSOIWIS, MCPSOIS, and HPSOIS, and the significance of the proposed methods is suggested as compared with these search methods.

On the other hand, when the sensing distance r exceeds 0.5 or more, it can be confirmed that the tracking performance of MPSOIWSIS, MCPSOSIS, and HPSOSIS becomes low and unstable. The tracking performance is relatively high within a certain range of the sensing distance r of the sensor. And when the number m of sensors exceeds 8, there is not much difference in the search ability of these methods themselves.

Second, computer experiments were carried out to handle the tracking problems of variable speed II type and variable speed III type. The obtained search results are shown in **Figures 8** and **9**, respectively.

By comparing the search results shown in **Figures 7–9**, it is clear that each proposed search method has high tracking ability in each case. As the main search characteristics, we can see that as the sensing distance r of the sensor increases and

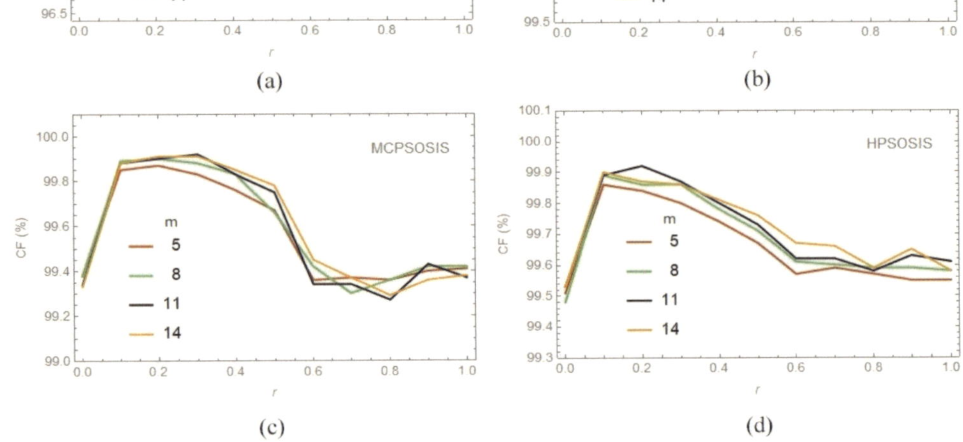

Figure 7.
Effect of handling the tracking problem of constant speed I type with adjustment of the number m and sensing distance r of sensors. (a) MPSOSIS case, (b) MPSOIWSIS case, (c) MCPSOSIS case, and (d) HPSOSIS case.

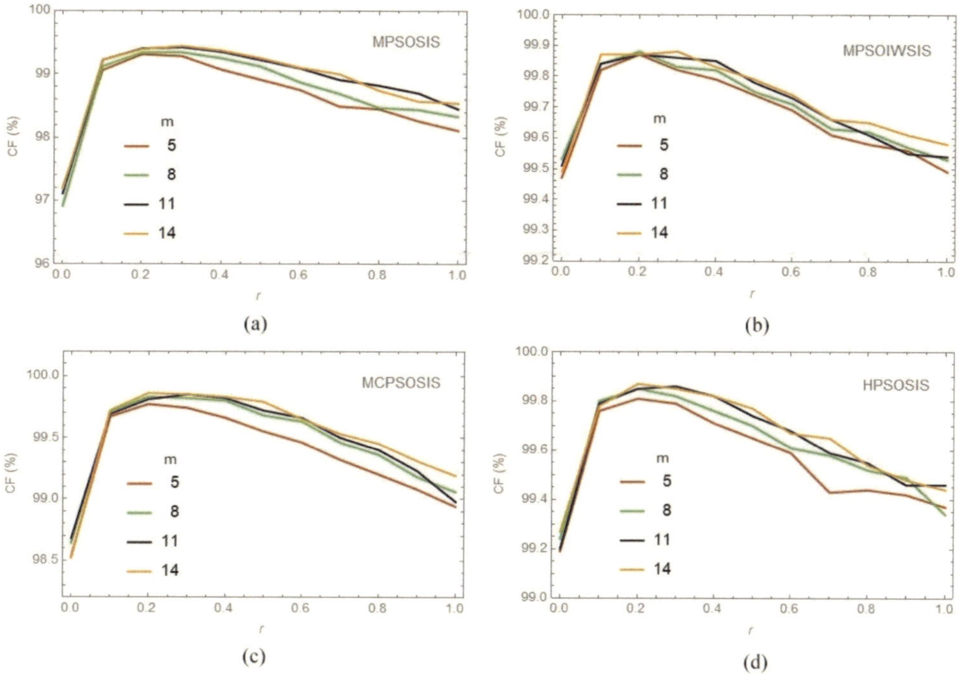

Figure 8.
Effect of handling the tracking problem of variable speed II type with adjustment of the number m and sensing distance r of sensors. (a) MPSOSIS case, (b) MPSOIWSIS case, (c) MCPSOSIS case, and (d) HPSOSIS case.

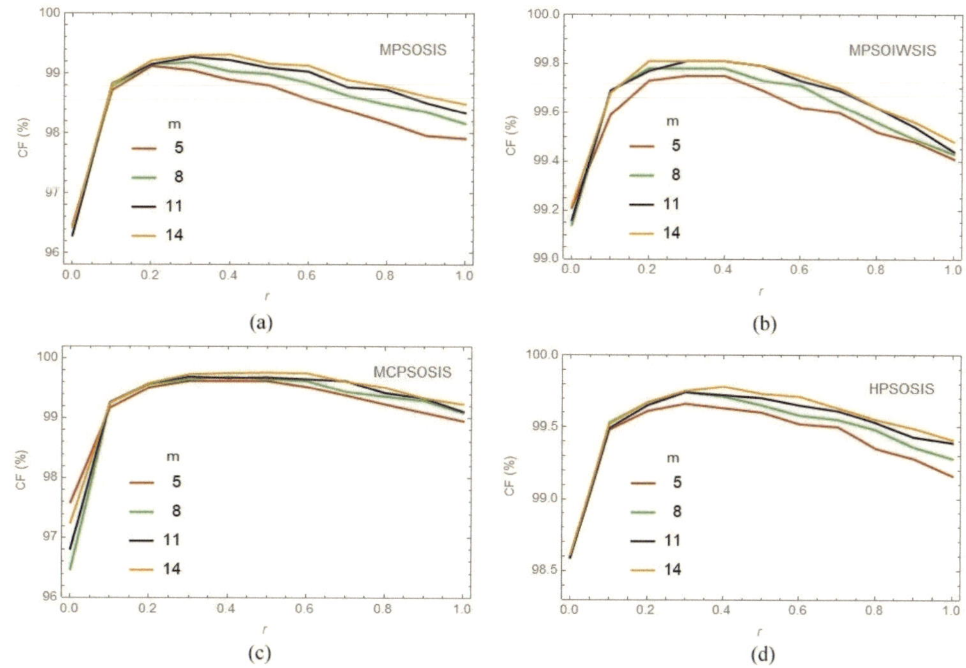

Figure 9.
Effect of handling the tracking problem of variable speed III type with adjustment of the number m and sensing distance r of sensors. (a) MPSOSIS case, (b) MPSOIWSIS case, (c) MCPSOSIS case, and (d) HPSOSIS case.

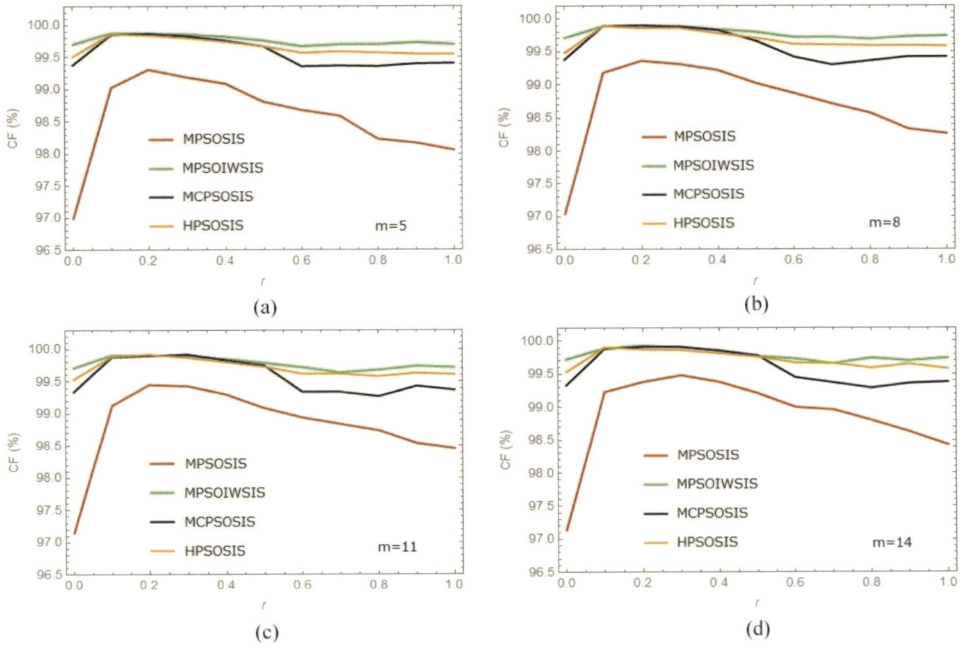

Figure 10.
Search ability of each proposed method for handling the tracking problem of constant speed I type. (a) m = 5 case, (b) m = 8 case, (c) m = 11 case, and (d) m = 14 case.

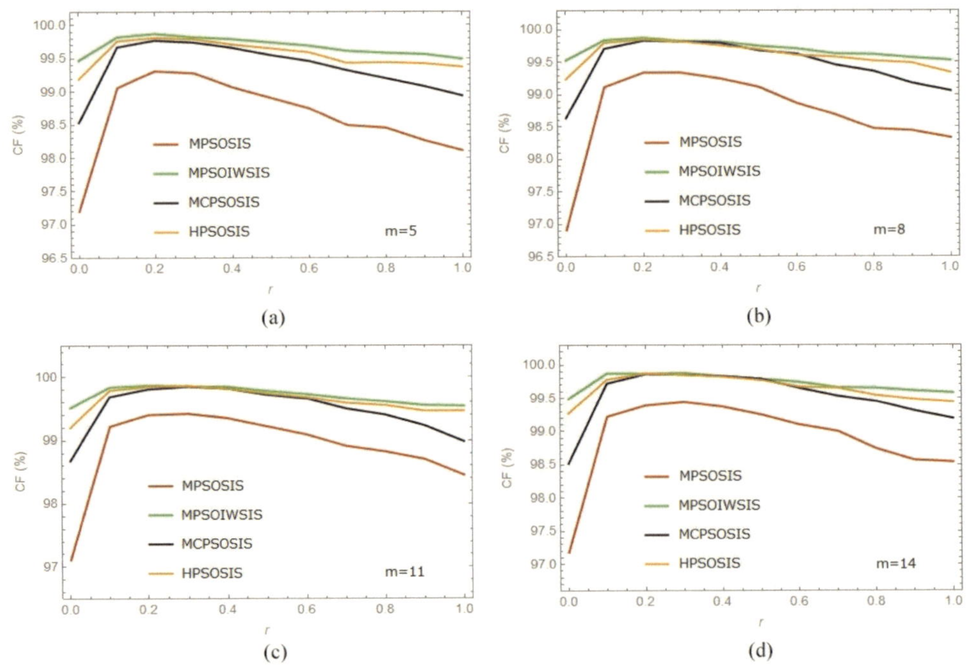

Figure 11.
Search ability of each proposed method for handling the tracking problem of variable speed type. (a) m = 5 case, (b) m = 8 case, (c) m = 11 case, and (d) m = 14 case.

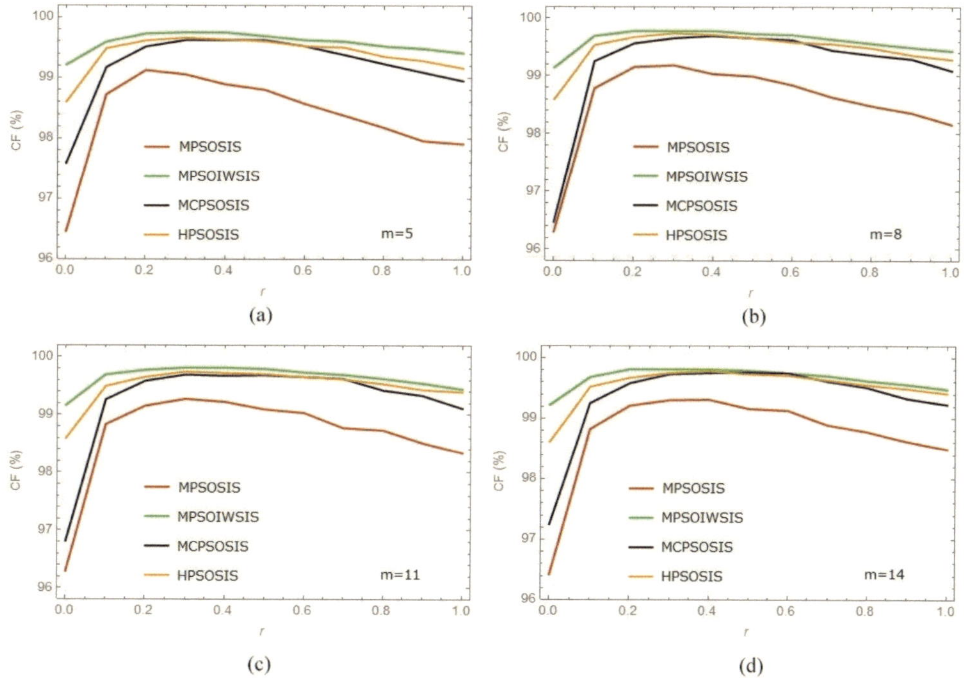

Figure 12.
Search ability of each proposed method for handling the tracking problem of variable speed III type. (a) m = 5 case, (b) m = 8 case, (c) m = 11 case, and (d) m = 14 case.

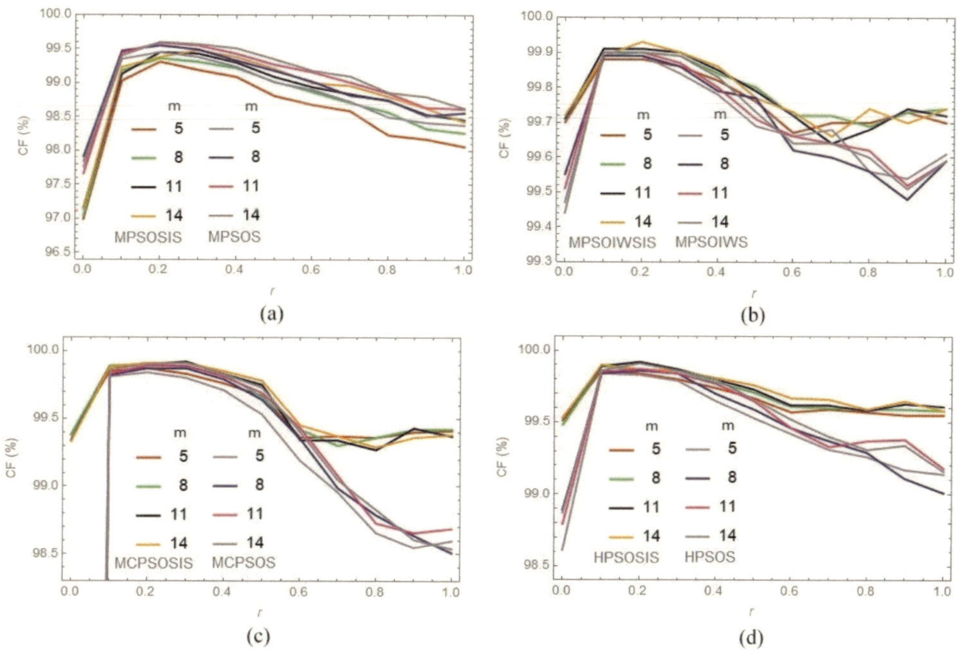

Figure 13.
The best and average solutions for handling the tracking problem of constant speed I type. (a) MPSOSIS and MPSOS case, (b) MPSOIWSIS and MPSOIWS case, (c) MCPSOSIS and MCPSOS case, and (d) HPSOSIS and HPSOS case.

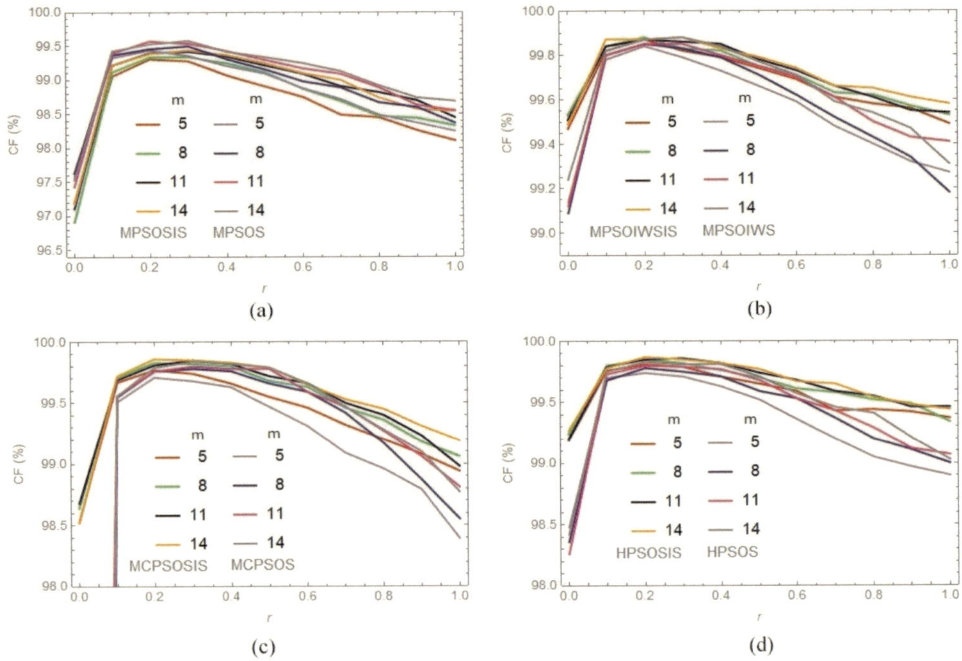

Figure 14.
The best and average solutions for handling the tracking problem of variable speed II type. (a) MPSOSIS and MPSOS case, (b) MPSOIWSIS and MPSOIWS case, (c) MCPSOSIS and MCPSOS case, and (d) HPSOSIS and HPSOS case.

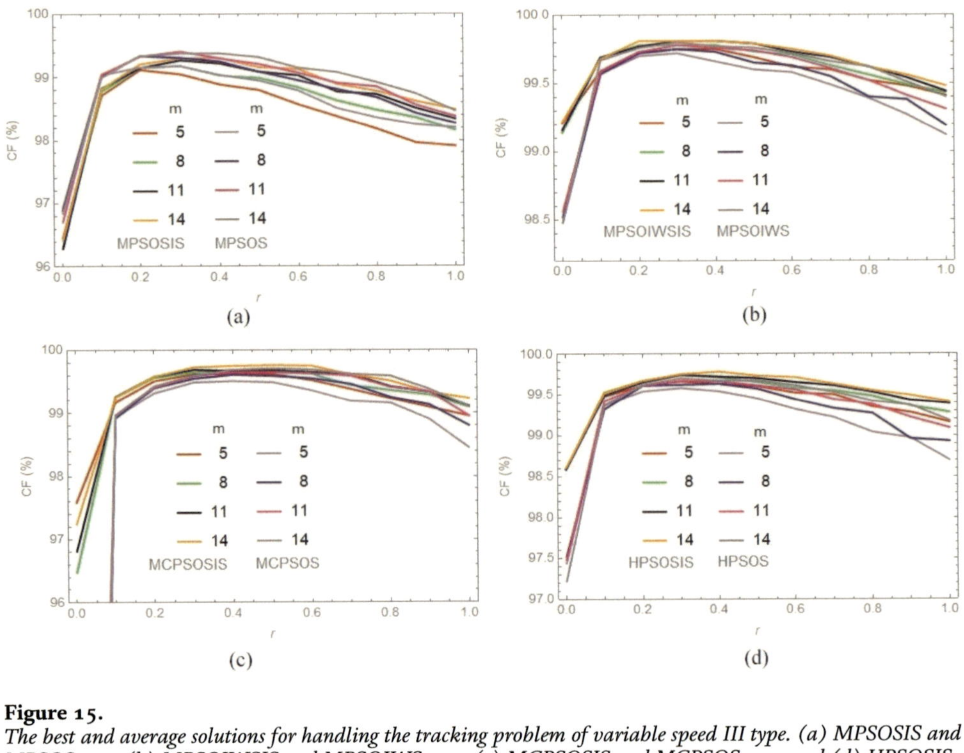

Figure 15.
The best and average solutions for handling the tracking problem of variable speed III type. (a) MPSOSIS and MPSOS case, (b) MPSOIWSIS and MPSOIWS case, (c) MCPSOSIS and MCPSOS case, and (d) HPSOSIS and HPSOS case.

the fitness value of the best solution gradually increases and gradually decays after passing through a certain peak value of the *CF*.

4.3 Performance comparison of the proposed methods

In this section, we compare the search performance of the four proposed methods, that is, MPSOSIS, MPSOIWSIS, MCPSOSIS, and HPSOSIS, by handling the same tracking problem. **Figure 10** shows the search results obtained by handling the tracking problem of constant speed I type.

We can see clearly that the search performance of MPSOSIS is the lowest regardless of the number of sensors used. For the remaining three proposed methods, that is, MPSOIWSIS, MCPSOSIS, and HPSOSIS, it is obvious that the search performance of MCPSOSIS is good within a certain range of the sensing distance r. Overall, it is clear that the search performance of MPSOIWSIS and HPSOSIS is relatively better in search ability. As the sensing distance r increases, all of their cumulative fitness values gradually decrease.

Similarly, **Figures 11** and **12** show the search results obtained by handling the tracking problems of variable speed II type and variable speed III type, respectively. Observing the obtained search results of both, it is almost the same as the finding obtained from the data analysis of the search result in **Figure 10**. In particular, it is found that the search performance of each proposed method is very lower when sensors are not used. In this case, the proposed methods (i.e., MPSOSIS, MPSOIWSIS, MCPSOSIS, and HPSOSIS) correspond to the existing methods (i.e., MPSOIS, MPSOIWIS, MCPSOIS, and HPSOIS). Thus, the important role of the used sensors is clearly shown.

4.4 Performance comparison without the strategy of information sharing

In order to investigate the effectiveness of the proposed methods under the situation of multiple particle swarm search, computer experiments on the existing search methods, that is, MPSOS, MPSOIWS, MCPSOS, and HPSOS, were implemented.

For intuitive comparison of both, the obtained results are shown in **Figures 13** and **15**, respectively. When there is no sensor, it is understood that the difference between them is the largest. It is also found that the attenuation of the cumulative fitness of the latter becomes relatively fast as the sensing distance r increases.

Except for the results in **Figures 13(a)**, **14(a)**, and **15(a)**, we discovered that the search results of the proposed methods, that is, MPSOIWSIS, MCPSOSIS, and HPSOSIS, are better than the existing methods, that is, MPSOIWS, MCPSOS, and HPSOS, except for the MPSOSIS case. Therefore, the effectiveness of the information sharing strategy is confirmed even in the case of multiple particle swarm search. The obtained results in **Figures 14** and **15** show that the attenuation of the existing methods becomes faster as r increases. However, with respect to handling the three kinds of tracking problems, further investigation and confirmation are required as to why the former's search results are generally lower in the maximum value of the cumulative fitness by the latter.

5. Conclusions and future research

In this chapter, we proposed the four new search methods, that is, MPSOSIS, MPSOIWSIS, MCPSOSIS, and HPSOSIS, to deal with dynamic optimization problems. For investigating and comparing their tracking ability and performance, we modified the number of sensors and adjusted the sensing distance to implement computer experiments. As the given tracking problems, we used a set of benchmark problems of constant speed I type, variable speed II type, and variable speed III type.

Computer experiments were carried out to handle each given tracking problem. Based on various experimental results obtained, the prominent search ability and performance of each proposed search method is confirmed.

Specifically, regarding search performance of the proposed methods, it is found that the obtained search results of MPSOIWSIS, MCPSOSIS, and HPSOSIS are better than the existing methods, that is, MPSOIWS, MCPSOS, HPSOS, MPSOIWIS, MCPSOIS, and HPSOIS. Also, in addition to enhancing the processing capacity for dealing with the given tracking problems, the efficiency of the search itself is also improved. However, in order to obtain good tracking ability and performance, it is necessary to select an appropriate value for the sensing distance of the sensor.

As future research subjects, based on the sensing information obtained from the sensors, we will advance the development of PMSO [22], that is, introducing the strategy of sharing information during the search and raising the intellectual level in particle multi-swarm search. Alternatively, the proposal methods utilizing the excellent tracking ability of MPSOIWSIS and HPSOSIS are applied extensively to dynamic search problems such as identification of control systems and recurrent network learning.

Author details

Hiroshi Sho
Department of Human Intelligence Systems, Kyushu Institute of Technology, Japan

*Address all correspondence to: zhang@brain.kyutech.ac.jp

References

[1] Gaing ZL. A particle swarm optimization approach for optimum design of PID controller in AVR system. IEEE Transations on Energey Conversion. 2004;**19**(2):384-391

[2] Gallego N, Mocholi A, Menendez M, Barrales R. Traffic monitoring: Improving road safety using a laser scanner sensor. In: Proceedings of Electronics, Robotic and Automotive Mechanics Conference (CERMA'09); Cuemavaca Morelos, Mexico. 2009. pp. 281-286

[3] Rai K, Seksena SBL, Thakur AN. A comparative performance analysis for loss minimization of induction motor drive based on soft computing techniques. International Journal of Applied Engineering Research. 2018; **13**(1):210-225

[4] Tehsin S, Rehman S, Saeed MOB, Riaz F, Hassan A, Abbas M, et al. Self-organizing hierarchical particle swarm optimization of correlation filters for object recognition. IEEE Access. 2017;**5**: 24495-24502. DOI: 10.1109/ACCESS. 2017.2762354

[5] Zhang Y, Wang S, Ji G. A comprehensive survey on particle swarm optimization algorithm and its applications. Hindawi Publish Corporation, Mathematical Problems in Engineering. 2015;**2015**:38. Article ID 931256. DOI: 10.1155/2015/931256

[6] Alam A, Dobbie G, Koh YS, Riddle P, Rehman SU. Research on particle swarm optimization based clustering: A systematic review of literature and techniques. Swarm and Evolutionary Computation, Elsevier. 2014;**17**(2014): 1-13. DOI: 10.1016/j.swevo.2014.02.001 [Accessed: February 8, 2019]

[7] Cui X, Potok TE. Distributed adaptive particle swarm optimizer in dynamic environment. In: IEEE International Parallel and Distributed Processing Symposium; Long Beach, CA. 2007. pp. 1-7

[8] Rezazadeh I, Meybodi MR, Naebi A. Adaptive particle swarm optimization algorithm for dynamic environment. In: 2011 Third International Conference on Computational Intelligence, Modelling & Simulation. 2011. pp. 120-129

[9] Spall JC. Stochastic optimization. In: Gentle J, et al. editors. Handbook of Computational Statistics. Heidelberg, Germany: Springer; 2004. pp. 169-197

[10] Xia X, Gui L, Zhan Z-H. A multi-swarm particle swarm optimization algorithm based on dynamical topology and purposeful detecting. Applied Soft Computing. 2018;**67**:126-140. Available from: https://www.sciencedirect.com/science/article/pii/S1568494618301017 [Accessed: February 6, 2019]

[11] Yu X, Estevez C. Adaptive multiswarm comprehensive learning particle swarm optimization. Information. 2018;**9**(173):15. DOI: 10.3390/info9070173 [Accessed: February 6, 2019]

[12] Fogel LJ, Owen AJ, Walsh MJ. On the evolution of artificial intelligence. In: Proceedings of the Fifth National Symposium on Human Factors in Electronics; San Diego, CA, USA; 1964. pp. 63-76

[13] Goldberg DE. Genetic Algorithm in Search Optimization and Machine Learning. Reading: Addison-Wesley; 1989

[14] Holland H. Adaptation in Natural and Artificial Systems. Ann Arbor, MI, USA: University of Michigan Press; 1975

[15] Reyes-Sierra M, Coello CAC. Multi-objective particle swarm optimizers:

A survey of the state-of-the-art. International Journal of Computational Intelligence Research. 2006;**2**(3): 287-308

[16] Blackwell TM. Swarms in dynamic environments. In: Proceedings of the 2003 Genetic and Evolutionary Computation Conference, LNCS; 2003. pp. 1-12

[17] Hu X, Eberhart RC. Adaptive particle swarm optimization: Detection and response to dynamic systems. In: Proceedings of the 2002 IEEE Congress on Evolutionary Computations, Vol. 2; Honolulu, HI, USA; 2002. pp. 1666-1670

[18] Sho H. The search feature of particle swarm optimizer with sensors in dynamic environment. IEICE Technical Report. 2017;**117**(63):77-82. (In Japanese)

[19] Sho H. Use of multiple particle swarm optimizers with sensors on solving tracking problems. IEICE Technical Report. 2018;**118**(7):9-14. (In Japanese)

[20] Zhang H. An analysis of multiple particle swarm optimizers with inertia weight for multi-objective optimization. IAENG International Journal of Computer Science. 2012;**39**(2):10

[21] Sho H. Particle multi-swarm optimization: A proposal of multiple particle swarm optimizers with information sharing. In: Proceedings of 2017 10th International Workshop on Computational Intelligence and Applications; Hiroshima, Japan; 2017. pp. 109-114. DOI: 10.1109/IWCIA.2017.8203570

[22] Sho H. Expansion of particle multi-swarm optimization. Artificial Intelligence Research. 2018;**7**(2):74-85. DOI: 10.5430/air.v7n2p74

[23] del Valle Y, Venayagamoorthy GK, Mohagheghi S, Hernandez JC, Harley RG. Particle swarm optimization: Basic concepts, variants and applications in power systems. IEEE Transactions on Evolutionary Computation. 2008;**12**(2): 171-195. DOI: 10.1109/TEVC.2007.896686

[24] Eberhart RC, Kennedy J. A new optimizer using particle swarm theory. In: Proceedings of the sixth International Symposium on Micro Machine and Human Science; Nagoya, Japan; 1995. pp. 39-43. DOI: 10.1109/MHS.1995.494215

[25] Kennedy J, Eberhart RC. Particle swarm optimization. In: Proceedings 1995 IEEE International Conference on Neural Networks; Perth, Australia; 1995. pp. 1942-1948

[26] Eberhart RC, Shi Y. Comparing inertia weights and constriction factors in particle swarm optimization. In: Proceedings of the 2000 IEEE Congress on Evolutionary Computation. Vol. 1; San Diego, CA; 2000. pp. 84-88. DOI: 10.1109/CEC.2000.870279

[27] Shi Y, Eberhart RC. A modified particle swarm optimiser. In: Proceedings of the IEEE International Conference on Evolutionary Computation; Anchorage, Alaska, USA; 1998. pp. 69-73. DOI: 10.1109/ICEC.1998.699146

[28] Clerc M, Kennedy J. The particle swarm-explosion, stability, and convergence in a multidimensional complex space. IEEE Transactions on Evolutionary Computation. 2000;**6**(1): 58-73. DOI: 10.1109/4235.985692

[29] Clerc M. Particle Swarm Optimization. UK: ISTE Ltd; 2006

[30] Trelea IC. The particle swarm optimization algorithm: Convergence analysis and parameter selection. Journal of Information Processing Letter. 2003;**85**:317-325. DOI: 10.1016/

S0020-0190(02)00447-7 [Accessed: December 11, 2018]

[31] Innocente MS, Sienz. Particle swarm optimization with inertia weight and constriction factor. In: Proceedings of International Conference on Swarm Intelligence; Cergy, France; 2011. pp. 1-11

[32] El-Abd M, Kamel MS. A taxonomy of cooperative particle swarm optimizers. International Journal of Computational Intelligence Research. 2008;**4**(2):137-144

[33] Sedighizadeh D, Mashian E. Particle swarm optimization networks, taxonomy and application. International Journal of Computer Theory and Engineering. 2009;**1**(5):486-502. DOI: 10.7763/IJCTE.2009.V1.80

[34] Zhang H. A new expansion of cooperative particle swarm optimization. In: Proceedings of the 17th International Conference on Neural Information Processing (ICONIP2010), Part I, LNCS 6443, Neural Information Processing—Theory and Algorithms; Sydney, Australia; 2010. pp. 593-600

Chapter 3

Particle Swarm Optimization: A Powerful Technique for Solving Engineering Problems

Bruno Seixas Gomes de Almeida and Victor Coppo Leite

Abstract

This chapter will introduce the particle swarm optimization (PSO) algorithm giving an overview of it. In order to formally present the mathematical formulation of PSO algorithm, the classical version will be used, that is, the inertial version; meanwhile, PSO variants will be summarized. Besides that, hybrid methods representing a combination of heuristic and deterministic optimization methods are going to be presented as well. Before the presentation of these algorithms, the reader will be introduced to the main challenges when approaching PSO algorithm. Two study cases of diverse nature, one regarding the PSO in its classical version and another one regarding the hybrid version, are provided in this chapter showing how handful and versatile it is to work with PSO. The former case is the optimization of a mechanical structure in the nuclear fuel bundle and the last case is the optimization of the cost function of a cogeneration system using PSO in a hybrid optimization. Finally, a conclusion is presented.

Keywords: PSO algorithm, hybrid methods, nuclear fuel, cogeneration system

1. Introduction

Maximizing earns or minimizing losses has always been a concern in engineering problems. For diverse fields of knowledge, the complexity of optimization problems increases as science and technology develop. Often, examples of engineering problems that might require an optimization approach are in energy conversion and distribution, in mechanical design, in logistics, and in the reload of nuclear reactors.

To maximize or minimize a function in order to find the optimum, there are several approaches that one could perform. In spite of a wide range of optimization algorithms that could be used, there is not a main one that is considered to be the best for any case. One optimization method that is suitable for a problem might not be so for another one; it depends on several features, for example, whether the function is differentiable and its concavity (convex or concave). In order to solve a problem, one must understand different optimization methods so this person is able to select the algorithm that best fits on the features' problem.

The particle swarm optimization (PSO) algorithm, proposed by Kennedy and Eberhart [1], is a metaheuristic algorithm based on the concept of swarm intelligence capable of solving complex mathematics problems existing in engineering [2]. It is of great importance noting that dealing with PSO has some advantages when compared with other optimization algorithms, once it has fewer parameters to adjust, and the ones that must be set are widely discussed in the literature [3].

2. Particle swarm optimization: an overview

In the early of 1990s, several studies regarding the social behavior of animal groups were developed. These studies showed that some animals belonging to a certain group, that is, birds and fishes, are able to share information among their group , and such capability confers these animals a great survival advantage [4]. Inspired by these works, Kennedy and Eberhart proposed in 1995 the PSO algorithm [1], a metaheuristic algorithm that is appropriate to optimize nonlinear continuous functions. The author derived the algorithm inspired by the concept of swarm intelligence, often seen in animal groups, such as flocks and shoals.

In order to explain how the PSO had inspired the formulation of an optimization algorithm to solve complex mathematical problems, a discussion on the behavior of a flock is presented. A swarm of birds flying over a place must find a point to land and, in this case, the definition of which point the whole swarm should land is a complex problem, since it depends on several issues, that is, maximizing the availability of food and minimizing the risk of existence of predators. In this context, one can understand the movement of the birds as a choreography; the birds synchronically move for a period until the best place to land is defined and all the flock lands at once.

In the given example, the movement of the flock only happens as described once all the swarm members are able to share information among themselves; otherwise, each animal would most likely land at a different point and at a different time. The studies regarding the social behavior of animals from the early 1990s stated before in this text pointed out that all birds of a swarm searching for a good point to land are able to know the best point until it is found by one of the swarm's members. By means of that, each member of the swarm balances its individual and its swarm knowledge experience, known as social knowledge. One may notice that the criteria to assess whether a point is good or not in this case is the survival conditions found at a possible landing point, such as those mentioned earlier in this text.

The problem to find the best point to land described features an optimization problem. The flock must identify the best point, for example, the latitude and the longitude, in order to maximize the survival conditions of its members. To do so, each bird flies searching and assessing different points using several surviving criteria at the same time. Each one of those has the advantage to know where the best location point is found until known by the whole swarm.

Kennedy and Eberhart inspired by the social behavior of birds, which grants them great surviving advantages when solving the problem of finding a safe point to land, proposed an algorithm called PSO that could mimic this behavior. The inertial version, also known as classical version, of the algorithm was proposed in 1995 [1]. Since then, other versions have been proposed as variations of the classical formulation, that is, the linear-decreasing inertia weight [5], the constriction factor weight [6], the dynamic inertia and maximum velocity reduction, also in Ref. [6], besides hybrid models [7] or even quantum inspired approach optimization techniques that can be applied to PSO [8]. This chapter will only present the inertial model of PSO, as it is the state-of-the-art algorithm, and to understand better the derivations of PSO, one should firstly understand its classical version.

The goal of an optimization problem is to determine a variable represented by a vector $X = [x_1 x_2 x_3 \dots x_n]$ that minimizes or maximizes depending on the proposed optimization formulation of the function $f(X)$. The variable vector X is known as position vector; this vector represents a variable model and it is n dimensions vector, where n represents the number of variables that may be determined in a problem, that is, the latitude and the longitude in the problem of determining a point to land by a flock. On the other hand, the function $f(X)$ is called fitness function or objective function, which is a function that may assess how good or bad a position X is, that is, how good a certain landing point a bird thinks it is after this animal finds it, and such evaluation in this case is performed through several survival criteria.

Considering a swarm with P particles, there is a position vector $X_i^t = (x_{i1}x_{i2}x_{i3}\dots x_{in})^T$ and a velocity vector $V_i^t = (v_{i1}v_{i2}v_{i3}\dots v_{in})^T$ at a t iteration for each one of the i particle that composes it. These vectors are updated through the dimension j according to the following equations:

$$V_{ij}^{t+1} = wV_{ij}^t + c_1r_1^t\left(pbest_{ij} - X_{ij}^t\right) + c_2r_2^t\left(gbest_j - X_{ij}^t\right) \quad (1)$$

and

$$X_{ij}^{t+1} = X_{ij}^t + V_{ij}^{t+1} \quad (2)$$

where i = 1,2, … ,P and j = 1,2, … ,n.

Eq. (1) denotes that there are three different contributions to a particle's movement in an iteration, so there are three terms in it that are going to be further discussed. Meanwhile, Eq. (2) updates the particle's positions. The parameter w is the inertia weight constant, and for the classical PSO version, it is a positive constant value. This parameter is important for balancing the global search, also known as exploration (when higher values are set), and local search, known as exploitation (when lower values are set). In terms of this parameter, one may notice that it is one of the main differences between classical version of PSO and other versions derived from it.

Velocity update equation's first term is a product between parameter w and particle's previous velocity, which is the reason it denotes a particles' previous motion into the current one. Hence, for example, if $w = 1$, the particle's motion is fully influenced by its previous motion, so the particle may keep going in the same direction. On the other hand, if $0 \le w < 1$, such influence is reduced, which means that a particle rather goes to other regions in the search domain. Therefore, as the inertia weight parameter is reduced, the swarm may explore more areas in the searching domain, which means that the chances of finding a global optimum may increase. However, there is a price when using lower w values, which is the simulations turn out to be more time consuming [1].

The individual cognition term, which is the second term of Eq. (1), is calculated by means of the difference between the particle's own best position, for example, $pbest_{ij}$, and its current position X_{ij}^t. One may notice that the idea behind this term is that as the particle gets more distant from the $pbest_{ij}$ position, the difference $\left(pbest_{ij} - X_{ij}^t\right)$ must increase; therefore, this term increases, attracting the particle to its best own position. The parameter c_1 existing as a product in this term is a positive constant and it is an individual-cognition parameter, and it weighs the importance of particle's own previous experiences. The other parameter that composes the product of second term is r_1, and this is a random value parameter with $[0, 1]$ range. This random parameter plays an important role, as it avoids premature convergences, increasing the most likely global optima [1].

Finally, the third term is the social learning one. Because of it, all particles in the swarm are able to share the information of the best point achieved regardless of which particle had found it, for example, $gbest_j$. Its format is just like the second term, the one regarding the individual learning. Thus, the difference $\left(gbest_j - X_{ij}^t\right)$ acts as an attraction for the particles to the best point until found at some t iteration. Similarly, c_2 is a social learning parameter, and it weighs the importance of the global learning of the swarm. And r_2 plays exactly the same role as r_1.

Lastly, **Figure 1** shows the PSO algorithm flowchart, and one may notice that the optimization logic in it searches for minimums and all position vectors are assessed by the function $f(X)$, known as fitness function. Besides that, **Figures 2** and **3** present the update in a particle's velocity and in its position at a t iteration, regarding a bi-dimensional problem with variables x_1 and x_2.

1. Initialization
   - 1.1. For each particle i in a swarm population size P:
     - 1.1.1. Initialize X_i randomly
     - 1.1.2. Initialize V_i randomly
     - 1.1.3. Evaluete the fitness $f(X_i)$
     - 1.1.4. Initialize $pbest_i$ with a copy of X_i
   - 1.2. Initialize $gbest$ with a copy of X_i with the best fitness
2. Repeat until a stopping criterion is satisfied:
   - 2.1. For each particle i:
     - 2.1.1. Update V_i^t and X_i^t according to Eqs. (1) and (2)
     - 2.1.2. Evaluete the fitness $f(X_i^t)$
     - 2.1.3. $pbest_i \longleftarrow X_i^t$ if $f(pbest_i) < f(X_i^t)$
     - 2.1.4. $gbest \longleftarrow X_i^t$ if $f(gbest) < f(X_i^t)$

Figure 1.
The PSO algorithm.

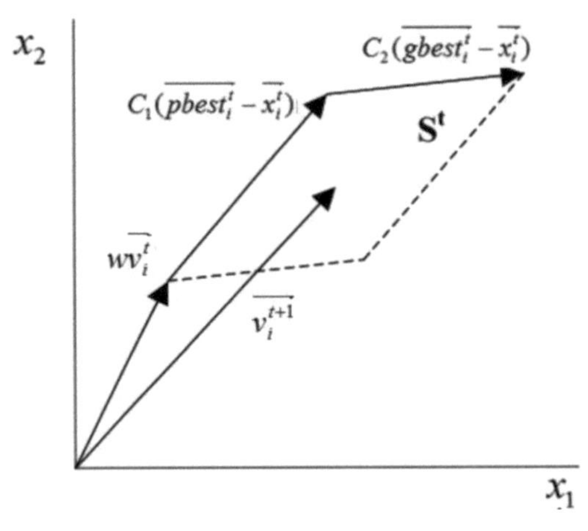

Figure 2.
The velocity vector at a t iteration as being composed by two components regarding a bi-dimensional problem.

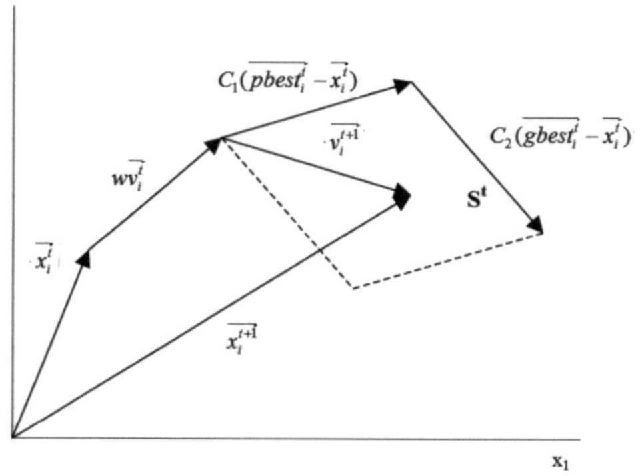

Figure 3.
The position vector being updated at a t iteration as being composed by two components regarding a bi-dimensional problem.

3. Hybrid methods: coupling PSO with deterministic methods

In general, optimization methods are divided into deterministic and heuristic. Deterministic methods aim to establish an iterative process involving a gradient, which, after a certain number of iterations, will converge to the minimum of the objective function. The iterative procedure of this type of method can be written as follows:

$$x^{k+1} = x^k + \alpha^k d^k \tag{3}$$

where x is the variable vector, α is the step size, d is the descent direction, and k is the iteration number. The best that can be expected from any deterministic gradient method is its convergence to a stationary point, usually a local minimum.

Heuristic methods, in contrast to deterministic methods, do not use the objective function gradient as a downward direction. Its goal is to mimic nature in order to find the minimum or maximum of the objective function by selecting, in an elegant and organized manner, the points where such a function will be calculated [9].

Hybrid methods represent a combination of deterministic and heuristic methods in order to take advantage of both approaches. Hybrid methods typically use a heuristic method to locate the most likely region where the global minimum is. Once this region is determined, the hybrid formulation algorithm switches to a deterministic method to get closer and faster to the minimum point. Usually, the most common approach used for this formulation is using the heuristic method to generate good candidates for an optimal solution and then using the best point found as a start point for the deterministic methods in order to converge to local minimums.

Numerous papers have been published over the last few years showing the efficiency and effectiveness of hybrid formulations [10–12]. There are also a growing number of publications over the last decade regarding hybrid formulations for optimization [13].

In this context, PSO algorithm can be combined with deterministic methods, increasing the chance of finding the function's most likely global optimal. This chapter presents the three deterministic methods in which the PSO was coupled: conjugate gradient method, Newton's method, and quasi-Newton method (BFGS). The formulation of each one of those is briefly presented in the following sections.

3.1 Conjugate gradient

The conjugate gradient method improves the convergence rate of the steepest descent method by choosing descending directions that are a linear combination of the gradient direction with the descending directions of previous iterations. Therefore, their equations are:

$$x^{k+1} = x^k + \alpha^k d^k \tag{4}$$

$$d^k = -\nabla\left(x^k\right) + \gamma^k d^{k-1} \tag{5}$$

where γ is the conjugation coefficient that acts by adjusting the size of the vectors. In the Fletcher-Reeves version, the conjugation coefficient is given by:

$$\gamma^k = \frac{\left\|-\nabla\left(x^k\right)\right\|^2}{\left\|-\nabla\left(x^{k-1}\right)\right\|^2} \tag{6}$$

3.2 Newton's method

While the steepest descent and conjugate gradient methods use first derivative information, Newton's method also uses second derivative information to accelerate the convergence of the iterative process. The algorithm used in this method is presented below:

$$x^{k+1} = x^k + \alpha^k d^k \tag{7}$$

$$d^k = -[H(x)]^{-1}\nabla U\left(x^k\right) \tag{8}$$

where $H(x)$ is the Hessian of the function. In general, this method requires few iterations to converge; however, it requires a matrix that grows with the size of the problem. If the estimate is far from the minimum, the Hessian matrix may be poorly conditioned. In addition, it involves inverting a matrix, which makes the method even more computationally expensive.

3.3 Quasi-Newton (BFGS)

BFGS is a type of quasi-Newton method. It seeks to approximate the inverse of the Hessian using the function's gradient information. This approximation is such that it does not involve second derivatives. Thus, this method has a slower convergence rate than Newton's methods, although it is computationally faster. The algorithm is presented below:

$$x^{k+1} = x^k + \alpha^k d^k \tag{9}$$

$$d^k = -H^k\nabla U\left(x^k\right) \tag{10}$$

$$H^k = H^{k-1} + M^{k-1} + N^{k-1} \tag{11}$$

$$M^{k-1} = \left[1 + \frac{\left(Y^{k-1}\right)^T.H^{k-1}.Y^{k-1}}{\left(Y^{k-1}\right)^T.d^{k-1}}\right]\frac{d^{k-1}.\left(d^{k-1}\right)^T}{\left(d^{k-1}\right)^T.Y^{k-1}} \tag{12}$$

$$N^{k-1} = -\left[\frac{d^{k-1}.\left(Y^{k-1}\right)^T.H^{k-1} + H^{k-1}.Y^{k-1}\left(d^{k-1}\right)^T}{\left(d^{k-1}\right)^T}\right] \tag{13}$$

$$Y^{k-1} = \nabla U\left(x^k\right) - \nabla U\left(x^{k-1}\right) \tag{14}$$

4. Recent applications and challenges

PSO can be applied to many types of problems in the most diverse areas of science. As an example, PSO has been used in healthcare in diagnosing problems of a type of leukemia through microscopic imaging [14]. In the economic sciences, PSO has been used to test restricted and unrestricted risk investment portfolios to achieve optimal risk portfolios [15].

In the engineering field, the applications are as diverse as possible. Optimization problems involving PSO can be found in the literature in order to increase the heat transfer of systems [16] or even in algorithms to predict the heat transfer coefficient [17]. In the field of thermodynamics, one can find papers involving the optimization of thermal systems such as diesel engine–organic Rankine cycle [18], hybrid diesel-ORC/photovoltaic system [19], and integrated solar combined cycle power plants (ISCCs) [20].

PSO has also been used for geometric optimization problems in order to find the best system configurations that best fit the design constraints. In this context, we can mention studies involving optical-geometric optimization of solar concentrators [21] and geometric optimization of radiative enclosures that satisfy temperature distribution and heat flow [22].

After having numerous versions of PSO algorithm such as those mentioned in the first section, PSO is able to deal with a broad range of problems, from problems with a few numbers of goals and continuum variables to others with challenging multipurpose problems with many discreet and/or continuum variables. Besides its potential, the user must be aware that the PSO will only achieve appreciated results if one implements an objective function capable of reflecting all goals at once. To derive such a function may be a challenging task that should require a good understanding of the physical problem to be solved and the ability to abstract ideas into a mathematical equation as well. The problems presented in the fourth section of this work provide examples of objective functions capable of playing this role.

Another challenge for one using PSO is how to handle the bounds of the search domain whenever a particle moves beyond it. Many popular strategies that had already been proposed are reviewed and compared for PSO classical version in [23]. Those strategies may be reviewed and understood by PSO users so this person can pick up the one that best fits the optimization problem features.

5. Engineering problems

In this chapter, two engineering problems will be described, one involving the fuel element of a nuclear power plant and the other involving a thermal cogeneration system. In the first problem, the traditional PSO formulation is used to find the optimal fuel element spacing. In the second problem, hybrid optimization algorithms are used to find the operating condition that minimizes total cost of operation of a cogeneration system.

5.1 Springs and dimples of a nuclear fuel bundle spacer grid

In [24], the authors perform the optimization of dimples and spring geometries existing in the nuclear fuel bundle (FB) spacer grid (SG). An FB is a structured group of fuel rods (FRs), and it is also known as fuel assembly, and on the other hand, an FR is a long, slender, zirconium metal tube containing pellets of fissionable material, which provide fuel for nuclear reactors [25]. An SG is a part of the nuclear fuel bundle and, **Figure 4** shows a schematic view of a nuclear FB; it is possible to see in this illustration how the FRs and the SGs are assembled together. In addition, **Figure 5** gives more details on how an SG's springs and dimples grip an FR, and **Figure 6** shows exactly what parts in the SG are the springs and the dimples that may be in contact with an FR. For this work, the PSO algorithm had been developed in MATLAB® (MathWorks Inc.); meanwhile, the mechanical calculations were performed with finite element analysis (FEA), using ANSYS 15.0 software.

The springs and the dimples act as supports required having special features once an FR releases a great amount of energy, caused by the nuclear reactions occurring within it. Hence, the material of an FR must face a broad range of temperatures when in operation; for example, around a variation of 300°C, this fact is an important matter for the springs and the dimples as those must not impose an

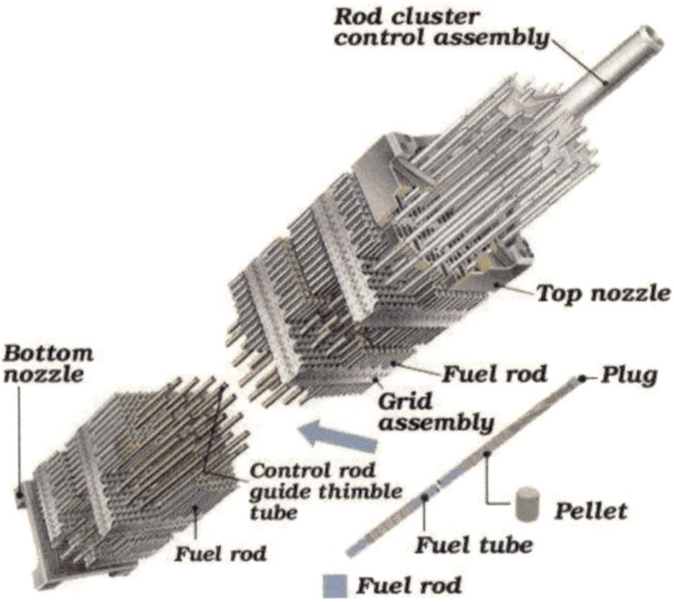

Figure 4.
A schematic view of a nuclear fuel bundle.

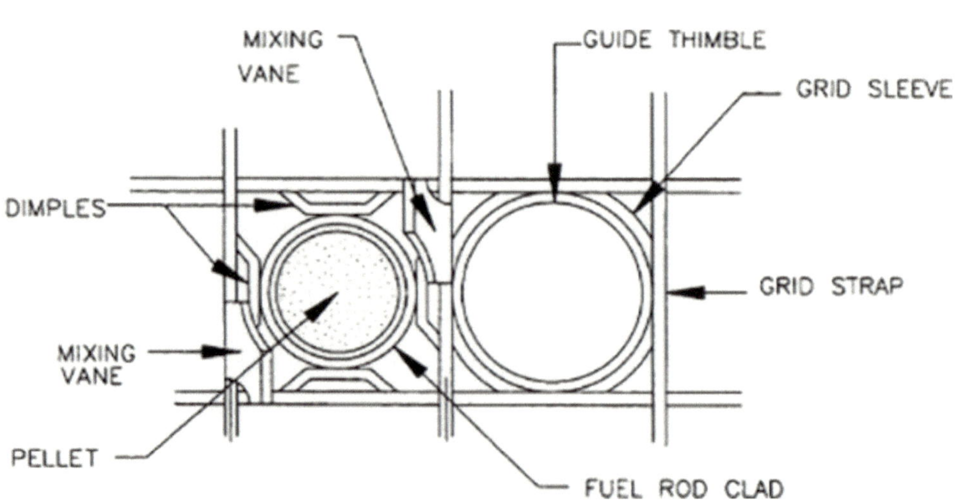

Figure 5.
The top view of a spacer grid gripping an FR through its dimples and springs.

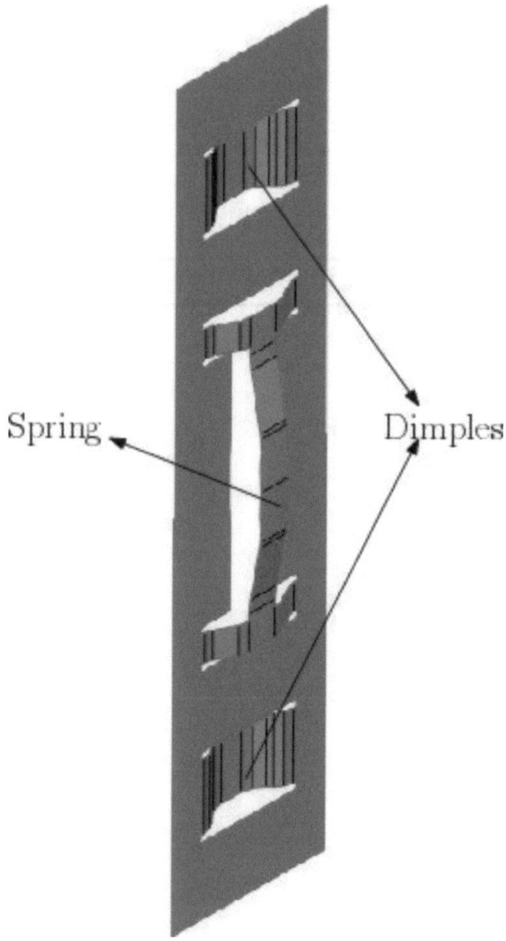

Figure 6.
A part of an SG strip with one spring and two dimples.

excessive gripping force on the rod, allowing it some axial thermal expansion. On the other hand, the upward water flow cooling the great amount of heat released by fission occurring within the rod creates a flow-induced vibration, so the springs and dimples must also limit the lateral displacement of the fuel rods. Besides that, the SG may also support the FRs through its dimples and springs at many loading conditions, that is, earthquakes and shipping and handling. To support safely the fuel in a nuclear reactor is an important matter during operation, and consequences such as the release of fission products from a fuel rod and a reactor safety shutdown could happen because of a poor design.

Finally, one can understand that as the springs and the dimples of an FB must have a geometry able to comply with conflicting requirements so the FRs remain laterally restrained, avoiding it from bowing and vibrating [26], using an optimization algorithm could be useful.

Jourdan et al. [13] had performed the optimization of the dimples and springs of an FB's SG using PSO classical version algorithm. The authors chose some geometry variables that should be important to features such as the gripping stiffness and the stress distribution in the spacer grid, which are the optimization goals in their work. Thus, the position vector is written as $X_i^t = (d_{i1}, d_{i2}, d_{i3}, d_{i4}, d_{i5}, d_{i6})^T$, and these lengths are those in **Figure 7**, while **Table 1** shows the range of such variables, that is, the search domain of the problem.

In PSO simulations from Ref. [24], for each position vector X_i^t, there is an FEA model with the geometry variable values of its related vector. In such FEA model, there are boundary conditions of an elastic static analysis. The boundary conditions considered in these simulations regard one spring and two dimples gripping two FRs, one in contact with the spring and the other one in contact with two dimples. Contacts were not modeled actually in order to simplify the model, and those were replaced by displacements similar to the condition of an FR with the diameter of 9.7 mm being gripped in the available space considering the X_i^t geometry. Other boundary conditions are also the restriction of translations and rotations on the welding nodes. **Figure 8** presents these boundary conditions regarding any position vector. All simulations were built using SHELL181 finite element [27], considering the material to be the Inconel 718.

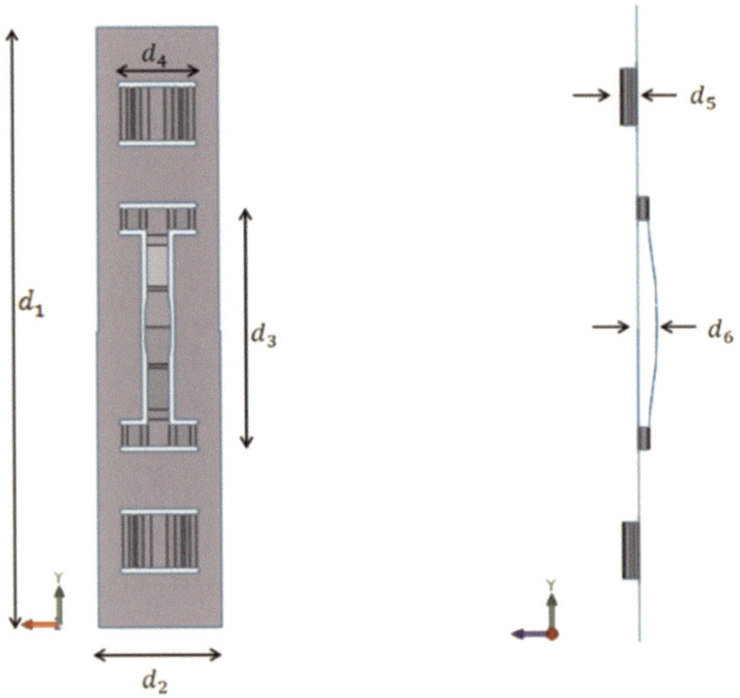

Figure 7.
Variable lengths that should feature the goals of the optimization.

Variable	Lower bound (mm)	Upper bound (mm)
d_1	50	70
d_2	10	15
d_3	5	30
d_4	5	10
d_5	1	5
d_6	1	5

Table 1.
Variable boundaries for the SG optimization.

The goals of the optimization performed in [24] are three: first, to minimize the stress intensity (SI) within the structure; second, to create an SG geometry featuring a gripping stiffness value as close as possible to some $K_{reference}$; and finally, to find a geometry that allows some axial thermal expiation by the FR. These three features are the main mechanical design requirements for an SG [26].

A simulation considering a population of $P = 100$ particles in a swarm and an inertial weight of $w = 0.3$ was performed in [26]. In order to obtain good results from PSO simulations, in other words, to determine the variable values that might fit on actual desired features, one must derive a fitness function able to properly grade all the optimization goals at once, without privileging none of the goals comparing to all others.

It should be noted that the grades assessed by the fitness function could be in an increasing scale or in a decreasing one, depending on the conception of the PSO algorithm. In [26], the authors chose to perform the search at a decreasing scale, and then the fitness function, Eq. (15), was designed to be minimized.

$$\begin{array}{ll} f(X) = \sigma + c_k\left(k_{calculated} - k_{reference}\right) & \text{if } displacement \geq 0.4mm \\ f(X) = 1,000,000 & \text{(otherwise)} \end{array} \tag{15}$$

The fitness function implemented assesses three different terms through two conditions. The two conditions regard the fact that the SG must allow some axial thermal expansion by the FR. To do so, a parameter *displacement* is created, and it measures the space that an FR with 9.7 mm diameter will use when gripped by an SG with some position vector geometry. Thus, a geometry producing a *displacement*

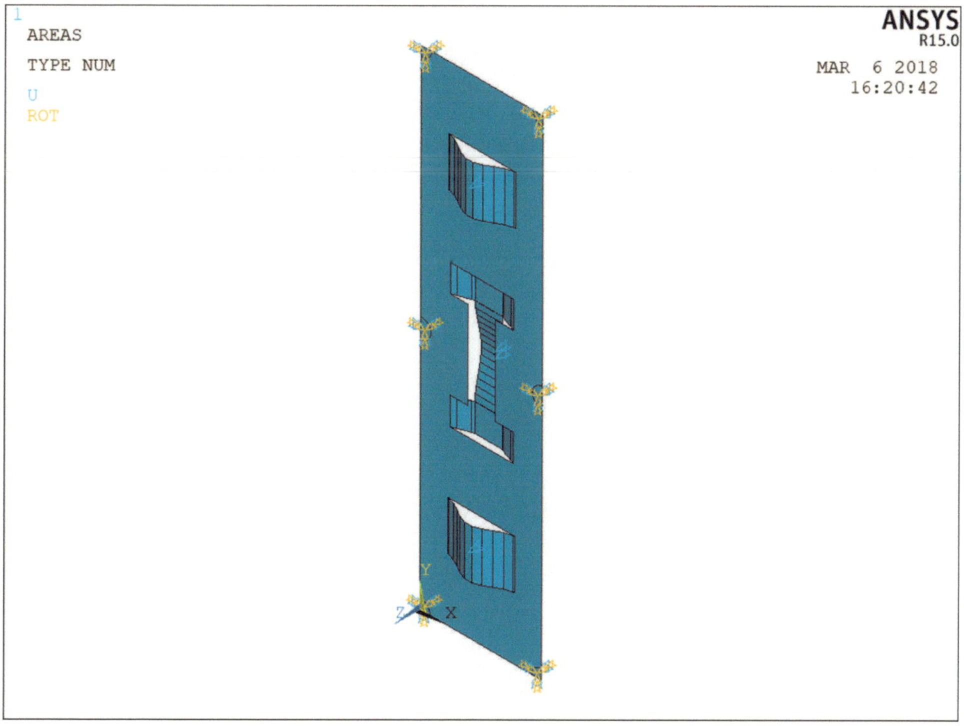

Figure 8.
Model's boundary condition considering any position vector.

over 0.4 mm will receive a high grade, meaning that this is an undesired feature, as the algorithm performs its optimization at a decreasing scale. The value of 0.4 mm is considered to be a good value for the design of an SG [28–31].

The σ parameter represents the SI, and then it is easy to understand that as the SI gets lower this term also does, which is desirable. Finally, the term $c_k(k_{calculated} - k_{reference})$ plays the role of finding a geometry that its stiffness, that is, $k_{calculated}$, gets as close as possible to a reference stiffness $k_{reference}$, where this last parameter is set to be 27.2 N/mm [31]. Meanwhile, the parameter c_k is a coefficient that must be set in order to fit the order of magnitude between the fitness function's terms, so none of them gets greater importance. In [24], c_k parameter had been calibrated by performing several PSO simulations, and then, this value was set to be 60. One should notice that the fitness function does not require a unit consistency, as its value is only a mathematical abstraction.

Figure 9 shows the fitness improvement performed to optimize the geometry of an SG's dimples and spring. This simulation resulted in an optimized geometry with an SI of 196 MPa and a gripping stiffness of 27.2 N/mm.

In [31], the authors performed an FEA and a real experiment to measure the SI and the gripping stiffness of the Chashma Nuclear Power Plant Unit 1's (CHASNUPP-1's) SG spring under the same conditions as considered in [24]. The results from [31] regarding a real SG that is in operation at CHASNUPP-1, which might not have been optimized, are 27.2 N/mm for the gripping stiffness and 816 MPa for the SI; meanwhile, the optimized result found in [24] has the same gripping stiffness although with an SI over 75% lower than CHASNUPP-1's SG. Thus, when comparing the results of the most likely optimal found using the PSO algorithm with those from a real SG [31], one can conclude that PSO had played its role well to design the component under study.

5.2 Cost of a cogeneration system

The second problem involves minimizing the function that represents the total cost of operation of a cogeneration system called CGAM. It is named after its creators (C. Frangopoulos, G. Tsatsaronis, A. Valero, and M. von Spakovsky) who

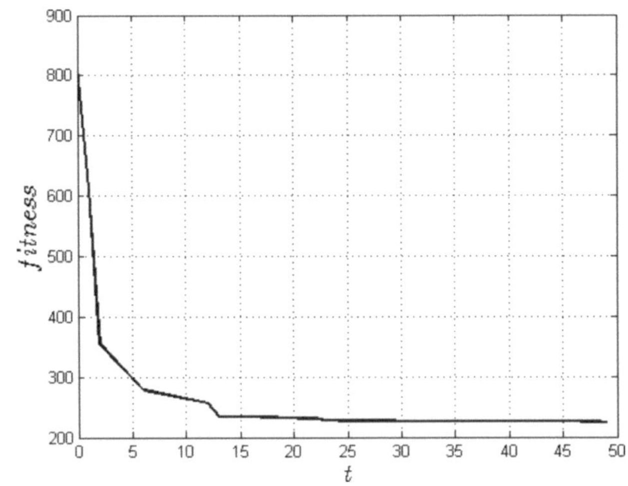

Figure 9.
Fitness improvements from simulation performed in [24].

decided to use the same system to compare the solution of the optimization problem with different methodologies [13]. **Figure 10** indicates the system.

The CGAM system is a cogeneration system consisting of an air compressor (AC), a combustion chamber (CC), a gas turbine (GT), an air preheater (APH), and a heat recovery steam generator (HRSG), which consists of an economizer for preheating water and an evaporator. The purpose of the cycle is the generation of 30 MW of electricity and 14 kg/s of saturated steam at a pressure of 20 bar.

The economic description of the system used in the present work is the same as the one adopted in the original work and considers the annual fuel cost and the annual cost associated with the acquisition and operation of each equipment. More details can be found in [32]. The equations for each component are presented below:

Air compressor:

$$Z_{AC} = \left(\frac{C_{11}\dot{m}_a}{C_{12} - \eta_{AC}}\right)\left(\frac{P_2}{P_1}\right)\ln\left(\frac{P_2}{P_1}\right) \tag{16}$$

Combustion chamber:

$$Z_{cc} = \left(\frac{C_{21}\dot{m}_a}{C_{22} - \frac{P}{P_3}}\right)\left[1 + \exp\left(C_{23}T_4 - C_{24}\right)\right] \tag{17}$$

Turbine:

$$Z_{GT} = \left(\frac{C_{31}\dot{m}_g}{C_{32} - \eta_{GT}}\right)\ln\left(\frac{P_4}{P_5}\right)\left[1 + \exp\left(C_{33}T_4 - C_{34}\right)\right] \tag{18}$$

Preheater:

$$Z_{APH} = C_{41}\left(\frac{\dot{m}_g(h_5 - h_6)}{(U)(\Delta TLM)}\right)^{0.6} \tag{19}$$

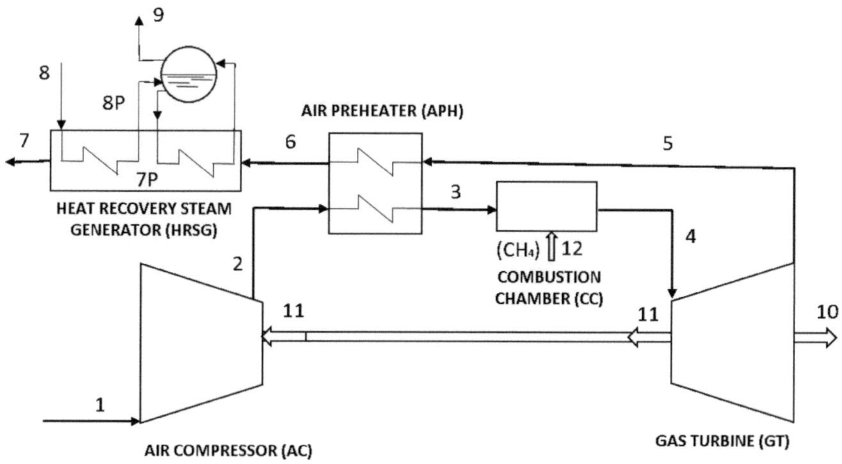

Figure 10.
CGAM system.

Heat recovery steam generator:

$$Z_{HRSG} = C_{51}\left(\left(\frac{Q_{PH}}{(\Delta TLM)_{PH}}\right)^{0.8} + \left(\frac{Q_{PH}}{(\Delta TLM)_{PH}}\right)^{0.8}\right) + C_{52}\dot{m}_{st} + C_{53}\dot{m}_g^{\ 1.2} \quad (20)$$

The general expression for the investment-related cost rate (\$/s) of each component is given by the following equation:

$$\dot{Z}_{i,invest} = \frac{Z_i \varphi CRF}{N.3600} \quad (21)$$

CRF is the capital recovery factor (18.2%), *N* is the number of annual plant-operating hours (8000 h), and φ is a maintenance factor (1.06). In addition, c_f is the fuel cost per unit of energy (0.004 \$/MJ). **Table 2** indicates the cost constants adopted for each component. The following equation represents the total cost of operation rate:

$$F = c_f \dot{m}_f PCI + \dot{Z}_{AC} + \dot{Z}_{APH} + \dot{Z}_{CC} + \dot{Z}_{GT} + \dot{Z}_{HRSG} \quad (22)$$

In order to perform the optimization of Eq. (22), the five decision variables adopted in the definition of the original problem are considered: the compression ratio (P_2/P_1), the isentropic efficiency of the compressor (η_{CA}), the isentropic efficiency of the turbine (η_{GT}), the air temperature at the preheater outlet (T_3), and the fuel gas temperature at the turbine inlet (T_4). To optimize the objective function, three optimization routines coupling PSO with different deterministic methods were used as indicated in **Table 3**.

Air compressor	$C_{11} = 39.5\ \$/\left(\frac{kg}{s}\right) C_{12} = 0.9$
Combustion chamber	$C_{21} = 25.6\ \$/\left(\frac{kg}{s}\right)\ C_{22} = 0.995$ $C_{23} = 0.018\ (K^{-1}) C_{24} = 26.4$
Gas turbine	$C_{31} = 266.3\ \$/\left(\frac{kg}{s}\right)\ C_{32} = 0.92$ $C_{33} = 0.036\ (K^{-1}) C_{34} = 54.4$
Preheater	$C_{41} = 39.5\ \$/(m^{1,2})\ U = 0.018 kW/(m^2K)$
HRSG	$C_{51} = 3650\ \$/\left(\frac{kW}{K}\right)^{0,8} C_{52} = 11,820\ \$/\left(\frac{kg}{s}\right)$ $C_{53} = 658\ \$/\left(\frac{kg}{s}\right)^{1,2}$

Table 2.
Cost constants.

	Heuristic	Deterministic
Hybrid 1	Particle swarm	Conjugate gradient
Hybrid 2	Particle swarm	Quasi-Newton
Hybrid 3	Particle swarm	Newton

Table 3.
Hybrid methods.

To solve the thermodynamic equations of the problem, the professional process simulator IPSEpro® version 6.0 was adopted. IPSEpro® is a process simulator used to model and simulate different thermal systems through their thermodynamic equations. This program was developed by SimTech and has a user-friendly interface, as well as a library with a wide variety of components, allowing the user to model and simulate conventional plants, cogeneration systems, cooling cycles, combined cycles, and more. The optimization method routines were written in MATLAB® (MathWorks Inc.), and the algorithm was integrated with IPSEpro® in order to solve the thermodynamic problem and perform the optimization.

To perform the optimization, the limits for the problem variables were established, as indicated in **Table 4** [33].

Table 5 presents the results found for the variables in each method and the value of the objective function. **Figures 11–13** present the graphs of the evolution of the cost function in relation to the function call for the performed optimizations.

In order to evaluate the algorithm's efficiency, a comparison was made between the results obtained in the present work and those obtained by [32, 33]. It is worth mentioning that the thermodynamic formulation used by [32] is slightly different from that constructed in the simulator; therefore, some differences in the final value of the objective function were already expected. In [33], the CGAM system was also built in IPSEpro® and the optimization was performed in MATLAB® using the following optimization methods: differential evolution (DE), particle swarm (PSO), simulated annealing (SA), genetic algorithm (GA), and direct pattern search (DPS). A comparison between the results is presented in **Figure 14**.

It is possible to verify that the hybrid methods used in this work have excellent performance, and the values found are compatible with the other references. This result consolidated the use of hybrid formulations used to optimize the objective function of the problem.

Limits
$7 \leq P_2/P_1 \leq 27$
$0.7 \leq \eta_{CA} \leq 0.9$
$0.7 \leq \eta_{GT} \leq 0.9$
$700\ K \leq T_3 \leq 1100\ K$
$1100\ K \leq T_4 \leq 1500\ K$

Table 4.
Variable limits.

	Hybrid 1	Hybrid 2	Hybrid 3
P_2/P_1	9.46	9.04	8.29
η_{CA}	0.83	0.83	0.85
T_3	600.43	612.53	606.47
η_{GT}	0.88	0.88	0.88
T_4	1210.95	1212.67	1214.65
Cost function ($/s)	0.33948	0.33953	0.33949

Table 5.
Optimization results.

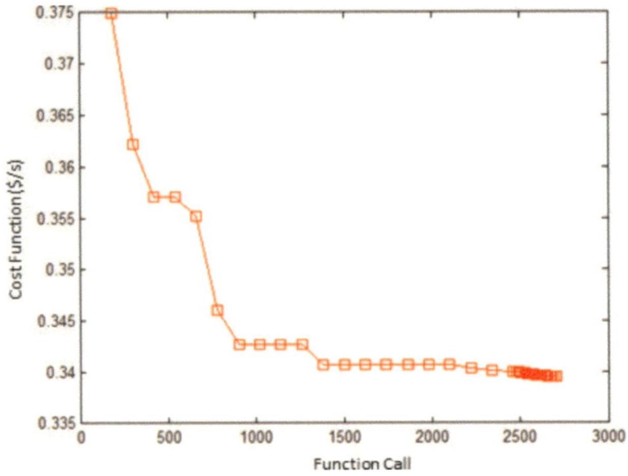

Figure 11.
Hybrid 1 optimization.

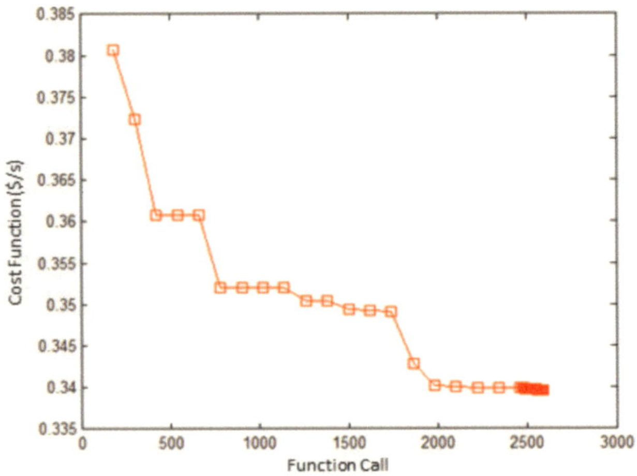

Figure 12.
Hybrid 2 optimization.

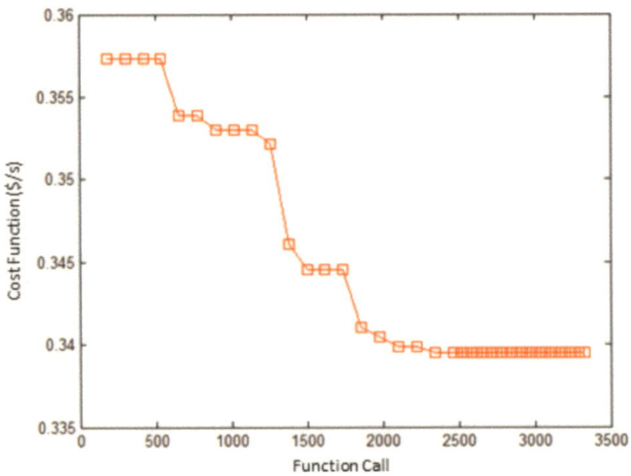

Figure 13.
Hybrid 3 optimization.

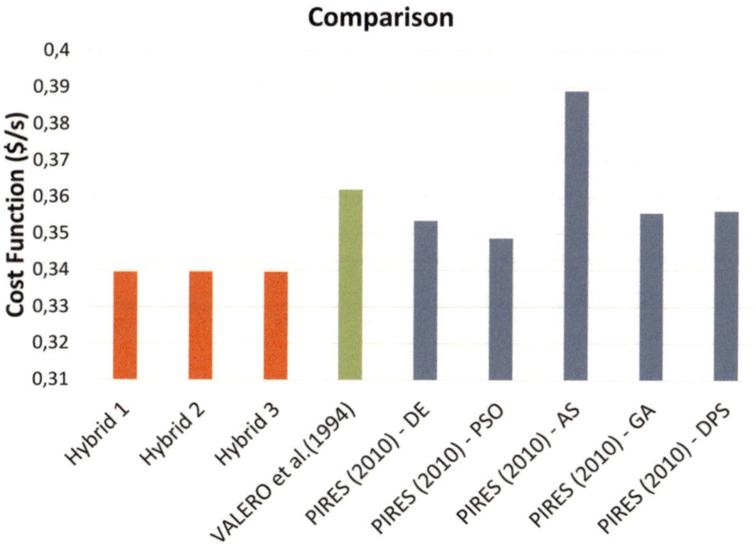

Figure 14.
Comparison between the results obtained and bibliographic references.

6. Conclusions

In the present work, it was possible to present the basic fundamentals involving the PSO method. The advantages and disadvantages of the method were discussed, as well as interpretations were provided to its algorithm. It was also possible to discuss about hybrid methods that combine deterministic and heuristic methods in order to extract the advantages of each one.

As discussed earlier, it is impracticable to say that the result obtained by an optimization method such as PSO is the global maximum or minimum, so some authors call the results as the most likely optimal global. Thus, some strategies can be employed in order to verify the validity of the optimal results obtained. One of the strategies is to compare with the results obtained by other optimization algorithms, as used in the present work. In the absence of optimal data available, due to either computational limitations or even lack of results of the subject, it is possible to use as strategy the comparison of information from real physical models, that is, that were not obtained through optimization algorithms, but instead good engineering practice and judgment gained through technical experience.

In addition, it was possible to apply the PSO algorithm to different engineering problems. The first involves the spacer grid of the fuel element and the second involves the optimization of the cost function of a cogeneration system. In both problems, satisfactory results were obtained demonstrating the efficiency of the PSO method.

Author details

Bruno Seixas Gomes de Almeida* and Victor Coppo Leite
Federal University of Rio de Janeiro, Rio de Janeiro, Brazil

*Address all correspondence to: brunoseixas@poli.ufrj.br

References

[1] Kennedy J, Eberhart RC. Particle swarm optimization. In: Proceedings of the International Conference on Neural Networks; Institute of Electrical and Electronics Engineers. Vol. 4. 1995. pp. 1942-1948. DOI: 10.1109/ICNN.1995.488968

[2] Meneses AAM, Machado MD, Schirru R. Particle swarm optimization applied to the nuclear reload problem of a pressurized water reactor. Progress in Nuclear Energy. 2009;**51**:319-326. DOI: 10.1016/j.pnucene.2008.07.002

[3] Sarkar S, Roy A, Purkayastha BS. Application of particle swarm optimization in data clustering: A survey. International Journal of Computers and Applications. 2013;**65**: 38-46. DOI: 10.5120/11276-6010

[4] Kennedy J, Eberhart RC. A new optimizer using particles swarm theory. In: Proceedings of Sixth International Symphosium on Micro Machine and Human Science IEEE. 1995. pp. 39-43. DOI: 10.1109/MHS.1995.494215

[5] Shi Y, Eberhart RC. Empirical study of particle swarm optimization. In: Proceedings of the 1999 IEEE Congress on Evolutionary Computation (CEC'99). Vol. 3. 1999. pp. 1945-1950. DOI: 10.1109/CEC.1999.785511

[6] Eberhart RC, Shi Y. Comparing inertia weights and constriction factors in particle swarm optimization. In: Proceedings of the 2000 Congress on Evolutionary Computation (CEC '00). Vol. 1. 2000. pp. 84-88. DOI: 10.1109/CEC.2000.870279

[7] Coelho L, Mariani VC. Particle swarm optimization with quasi-Newton local search for solving economic dispatch problem. In: IEEE International Conference on Systems, Man and Cybernetics, 2006. SMC '06. Vol. 4. 2006. pp. 3109-3113. DOI: 10.1109/ICSMC.2006.384593

[8] Han KH, Kim JH. Quantum-inspired evolutionary algorithm for a class of combinatorial optimization. IEEE Transactions on Evolutionary Computation. 2002;**6**:580-593. DOI: 10.1109/TEVC.2002.804320

[9] Colaço MJ, Orlande HRB, Dulikravich GS. Inverse and optimization problems in heat transfer. Journal of the Brazilian Society of Mechanical Sciences and Engineering. 2006;**28**:1-24. DOI: 10.1590/S1678-58782006000100001

[10] Nery RS, Rolnik V. Métodos Híbridos para Otimização global não-linear. In: Congresso Nacional de Matemática Aplicada e Computacional; Florianópolis, SC, Brasil. 2007

[11] Zadeh PM, Sokhansefat T, Kasaeian AB, et al. Hybrid optimization algorithm for thermal analysis in a solar parabolic trough collector based on nanfluid. Energy. 2015;**82**:857-864. DOI: 10.1016/j.energy.2015.01.096

[12] Dominkovic DF, Cosic B, Medic B, et al. A hybrid optimization model of biomass trigeneration system combined with pit thermal energy storage. Energy Conversion and Management. 2015;**104**: 90-99. DOI: 10.1016/j.enconman.2015.03.056

[13] Jourdan L, Basseur M, Talbi EG. Hybridizing exact methods and metaheuristics: A taxonomy. European Journal of Operational Research. 2009; **199**:620-629. DOI: 10.1016/j.ejor.2007.07.035

[14] Srisukkham W, Zhang L, Neoh SC, Todryk S, Lim CP. Intelligent leukaemia diagnosis with bare-bones PSO based feature optimization. Applied Soft

Computing. 2017;**56**:405-419. DOI: 10.1016/j.asoc.2017.03.024

[15] Zhu H, Wang Y, Wang K, Chen Y. Particle swarm optimization (PSO) for the constrained portfolio. Expert System with Applications. 2011;**38**:10161-10169. DOI: 10.1016/j.eswa.2011.02.075

[16] Payan S, Azimifar A. Enhancement of heat transfer of confined enclosures with free convection using blocks with PSO algorithm. Applied Thermal Engineering. 2016;**101**:79-91. DOI: 10.1016/j.applthermaleng.2015.11.122

[17] Malekan M, Khosravi A. Investigation of convective heat transfer of ferrofluid using CFD simulation and adaptive neuro-fuzzy inference system optimized with particle swarm optimization algorithm. Powder Technology. 2018;**333**:364-376. DOI: 10.1016/j.powtec.2018.04.044

[18] Zhao R, Zhang H, Song S, Yang F, Hou X, Yan Y. Global optimization of the diesel engine–organic Rankine cycle (ORC) combined system based on particle swarm optimizer (PSO). Energy Convesion and Management. 2018;**174**: 248-259. DOI: 10.1016/j.enconman. 2018.08.040

[19] Nogueira ALN, Castellanos LSM, Lora EES, Cobas VRM. Optimum design of a hybrid diesel-ORC/photovoltaic system using PSO: Case study for the city of Cujubim, Brazil. Energy. 2018; **142**:33-45. DOI: 10.1016/j.energy.2017. 10.012

[20] Mabrouk MT, Kheiri A, Feidt M. A systematic procedure to optimize integrated solar combined cycle power plants (ISCCs). Applied Thermal Engineering. 2018;**136**:97-107. DOI: 10.1016/j.applthermaleng.2018.02.098

[21] Ajdad H, Baba YF, Mers AA, Merron O, Bouatem A, Boutmmachte N. Particle swarm optimization algorithm for optical-geometric optimization of linear fresnel solar concentrators. Renewable Energy. 2019;**130**:992-1001. DOI: 10.1016/j.renene.2018.07.001

[22] Farahmand A, Payan S, Sarvari SMH. Geometric optimization of radiative enclosures using PSO algorithm. International Jounal of Thermal Sciences. 2012;**60**:61-69. DOI: 10.1016/j.ijthermalsci.2012.04.024

[23] Padhye N, Mittal P, Deb K. Boundary handling approaches in particle swarm optimization. Advances in Intelligents Systems and Computing. 2013;**201**:287-298. DOI: 10.1007/978-81-322-1038-2_25

[24] Leite VC, Schirru R, Neto MM. Particle swarm optimization applied to the nuclear fuel bundle spacer grid spring design. Nuclear Technology. 2018;**205**:637-645. DOI: 10.1080/ 00295450.2018.1516056

[25] United States Nuclear Regulatory Commission (U.S.NRC). Glossary. Available from: https://www.nrc.g ov/reading-rm/basic-ref/glossary [Accessed: 2019-06-14]

[26] United States Nuclear Regulatory Commission (U.S.NRC). Westinghouse AP1000 Design Control Document. Final safety analysis report. Westinghouse Electric Company; 2011

[27] ANSYS User's Manual for Revision 5.0. Swanson Analysis System, Inc.; 2013

[28] Shin MK et al. Optimization of a nuclear fuel spacer grid spring using homology constraints. Nuclear Engineering and Design. 2008;**238**: 2624-2634. DOI: 10.1016/j. nucengdes.2008.04.003

[29] Lee S, Kim Y, Song K. Parameter study for a dimple location in a space grid under the critical impact load. Journal of Mechanical Science and

Technology. 2008;**22**:2024-2029. DOI: 10.1007/s12206-008-0620-5

[30] Park KJ et al. Design of a spacer grid using axiomatic design. Journal of Nuclear Science and Technology. 2003; (12):989-997. DOI: 10.3327/jnst.40.989

[31] Wassen W et al. Fuel rod-to-support contact pressure and stress measurement for CHASNUPP-1 (PWR) fuel. Nuclear Engineering and Design. 2011;**241**:32-38. DOI: 10.1016/j.nucengdes.2010.11.004

[32] Frangopoulos C, Tsatsaronis G, Valero A, et al. CGAM problem: Definition and conventional solution. Energy. 1994;**19**:279-286. DOI: 10.1016/0360-5442(94)90112-0

[33] Pires TS. Método de Superfície de Resposta Aplicado à Otimização Termoeconômica de Sistemas de Cogeração Modelados em um Simulador de Processos [thesis]. Rio de Janeiro, Brasil: COPPE-UFRJ; 2010

Chapter 4

Feature Selection for Classification with Artificial Bee Colony Programming

Sibel Arslan and Celal Ozturk

Abstract

Feature selection and classification are the most applied machine learning processes. In the feature selection, it is aimed to find useful properties containing class information by eliminating noisy and unnecessary features in the data sets and facilitating the classifiers. Classification is used to distribute data among the various classes defined on the resulting feature set. In this chapter, artificial bee colony programming (ABCP) is proposed and applied to feature selection for classification problems on four different data sets. The best models are obtained by using the sensitivity fitness function defined according to the total number of classes in the data sets and are compared with the models obtained by genetic programming (GP). The results of the experiments show that the proposed technique is accurate and efficient when compared with GP in terms of critical features selection and classification accuracy on well-known benchmark problems.

Keywords: feature selection, classification algorithms, evolutionary computation, genetic programming, artificial bee colony programming

1. Introduction

In recent years, data learning and feature selection has become increasingly popular in machine learning researches. Feature selection is used to eliminate noisy and unnecessary features in collected data that can be expressed more reliably and high success rates are obtained in classification problems. There are several works which related to solve genetic programming (GP) in feature selected classification problem [1–4]. Since artificial bee colony programming (ABCP) is a recently proposed method, there is no work related to this field. In this chapter, we evaluated the success of classification by selecting the features of GP and ABCP automatic programming methods using different data sets.

1.1 Goals

The goal of this chapter is classify models are obtained with comparable accuracy to alternative automatic programming methods. The overall goals of chapter are set out below.

1. Evaluation of the performance of models with parameters such as classification accuracy, complexity.

2. Whether ABCP method actually can select related/linked features.

3. Evaluating training performance of automatic programming methods to determine if there is overfitting.

The organization of the chapter is as follows: background is described in Section 2, detailed description of GP and ABCP is introduced in Section 3. Then, experiments and results are presented and discussed in Section 4. The chapter is concluded in Section 5 with summarizing the observations and remarking the future work.

2. Background

2.1 Feature selection

Feature selection makes it possible to obtain more accurate results by removing irrelevant and disconnected features in model prediction. The model prediction provides the functional relationship between the output parameter y and the input parameters x of the data set. Removing irrelevant features reduces the dimension of the model, thus it reduces space complexity and computation time [5, 6].

Feature selection methods are examined in three main categories as filter methods, embedded methods and wrapper methods [7, 8]. Filtering methods evaluate features with the selection criterion based on correlations between features (feature relevance) and redundancy and associate of features with class label vectors. Wrapper methods take into account the success of classification accuracy and decide whether or not an object will be included in the model. In order to obtain the successful model, it is not preferred in time constrained problems because the data set is trained and tested many times [9]. Embedded methods perform feature selection as part of model construction is based on identifying the best divisor.

In recent years, increasing interest in discovering potentially useful information has led to feature selection researches [10–15]. In [10], a spam detection method of binary PSO with mutation operator (MBPSO) was proposed to reduce the spam labeling error rate of non-spam email. The method performed more successful than many other heuristic methods such as genetic algorithm (GA), particle swarm optimization (PSO), binary particle swarm optimization (BPSO), and ant colony optimization (ACO). Sikora and Piramuthu suggested GA for feature selection problem using Hausdorff distance measure [11]. GA was quite successful the accuracy of prediction accuracy and computational efficiency in real data mining problems. In [12], a wrapper framework was proposed to find out the number of clusters in conjunction in the selection of features for uncontrolled learning and normalize the tendencies of feature selection criteria according size. Feature subset selection using expectation maximization clustering (FSSEM) was used as the performance criterion for the maximum likelihood. Schiezaro and Pedrini proposed a feature selection method based on artificial bee colony (ABC) [13]. The method presented better results for the majority of the data sets compared to ACO, PSO, and GA. Yu et al. showed that selecting the discriminative genes of GP and expressing the relationships between the genes as mathematical equations were proof that GP has been applied feature selector and cancer classifier [2]. Landry et al. compared k-nearest neighbor (k-NN) with decision trees generated by GP in several benchmark datasets [14]. GP was more reliable performance for feature selection and classification problems. Our chapter is the first to work with the ABCP's ability to select the necessary features in datasets.

2.2 Classification

Classification provides a number of benefits to make it easier to learn about data and to monitor the data. Several researches have been applied to solve the classification problems [15–17]. Fidelis et al. classified each chromosome based on GA that represented classification rules [15]. The algorithm was evaluated in different data sets and achieved successful results. A new algorithm was proposed to learn the distance measure for the closest neighbor classifier for k-nearest multi class classification in [16]. Venkatesan et al. proposed progressive technique for multi class classification can learn new classes dynamically during the run [17].

Much work has been devoted to classification using GP and ABC [18–25]. GP based feature selection age layered population structure as a new algorithm for feature selection with classification was compared with other GP versions in [18]. Lin et al. proposed the feature layered genetic programming method for feature selection and feature extraction [19]. The method, had a multilayered architecture, was built using multi population genetic programming. The experimental results show that the method achieved high success in both feature selection and feature extraction as well as classification accuracy. Ahmed et al. aimed at automatic feature selection and classification of mass spectrometry data with very high specificity and small sample representation using GP [20]. GP achieved higher success as a classification method by selecting fewer features than other conventional methods. Liu et al. designed a new GP based ensemble system to classify different cancer types where the system was used to increase the diversity of each ensemble system [21]. ABC was used data clustering on benchmark problems and was compared conventional classification techniques in [22]. Karaboga et al. applied ABC on training feed forward neural networks and classified different datasets [23]. ABC was used to improve the performance of classification in several domains avoiding the issues related to band correlation in [24]. Chung et al. proposed ABC as a new tool for data mining particularly in classification and compared evolutionary techniques, standard algorithms such as naive Bayes, classification tree and nearest neighbor (k-NN) [25]. Works showed that GP and ABC are successful in classification area. In this chapter is the first work to compare GP and recently proposed ABCP method in feature selected classification.

3. GP and ABCP

This section explicitly details GP and ABCP automatic programming methods.

3.1 GP

GP, most well-known method, was developed by Koza [26]. GP has been applied to solve numerous interesting problems [27–29]. The basic steps for the GP algorithm are similar to the steps of genetic algorithm (GA) and use the same analogy as GA. The most important difference GP and GA is representation of individuals. While GA express individuals as fixed code sequences, GP express them as parse trees. Flow chart of GP is given in **Figure 1** [30].

The first step in the flow chart is the creation of the initial population. Each individual in the population is represented by a tree where each component is called

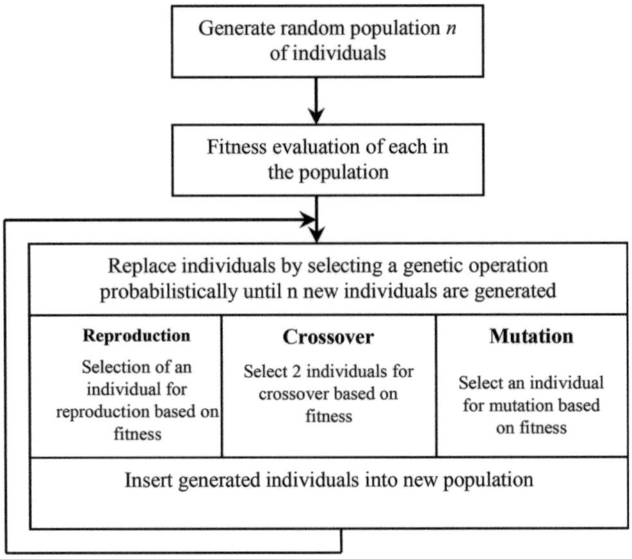

Figure 1.
The flow chart of GP.

node. The production of tree nodes is provided by terminals (constants or variables such as x, y, 5) and functions (arithmetic operators such as +, −/, sin, cos). Individuals are produced by the full method, the grow method, or the ramped half and half method [31]. Individuals are evaluated predetermined objective function. GP aims to increase the number of individuals with high quality survival and to decrease the number of low quality individuals. Individuals with high quality are more likely to pass on to the next generation. Individuals are developed them with exchange operators such as reproduction, crossover and mutation. Choosing the best individuals according to fitness are applied with methods like tournament, roulette wheel [32]. The crossover operator allows hybrid of two selected individuals to produce a new individual. Generally, sub-trees taken from two crossing points selected from parent trees are crossed to obtain new hybrid trees. The mutation operator provides unprecedented and unexplored individual elements [33]. Substitution of randomly selected tree instead of randomly selected node in the tree is called subtree mutation. Another method of mutation is a single point mutation. In this method, if the terminal is selected randomly from the tree, it is changed with the value selected from the terminal set. If the function is selected randomly from the tree, the value is selected from the function set. The best individuals of the previous generation are transferred to the current generation with elitism operator. The program is terminated when it is reached according to predefined stopping criteria such as the specific fitness value of the individuals, the number of generations.

3.2 ABCP

ABC algorithm was developed by Karaboga, modeling the food source search the intelligent foraging behavior of a honey bee swarm [34]. ABCP that was inspired ABC was introduced first time as a new method on symbolic regression [35]. In ABC, the positions of the food sources, i.e., solutions, are carried out with fixed size arrays and displays the values found by the algorithm for the predetermined variables as in GA. In the ABCP method, the positions of food sources are expressed in tree structure that is composed of different combinations of terminals and functions that are specifically defined for problems. The mathematical relationship of the solution model in ABCP can be represented the individuals in **Figure 2** is described Eq. (1). In these notations, x is used to represent the independent, and $f(x)$ is dependent variable.

$$f(x) = 3.75\pi x - (\log 5 - \sin(2y)) \quad (1)$$

In the ABCP model, the position of a food source is defined as a possible solution and nectar of the food source is defined for the quality of the solution. There are three different types of bees, as in the ABC: employed bee, onlooker bee and scout bee in the ABCP algorithm. Employed bees are responsible for bringing the hive of nectar from specific sources that have been previously discovered and they share information about the quality of the source with the onlooker bees. Every food source is visited by one employed bee who then takes nectar to hive. The onlooker bees monitor the employed bees in hives and turn to a new source using the information shared by the employed bees. After employed and onlooker bees complete the search processes, source are checked whether source nectars are exhausted. If a source is abandoned, the employed bee using the source becomes the scout bee and randomly searches for new sources. The main steps of ABCP algorithm is given in the flow chart of ABCP algorithm in **Figure 3**.

In ABCP, the production of solutions and the determination of the quality of solutions are carried out in a similar way to GP. In the initialization of the algorithm, solutions are produced by the full method, the grow method, or the ramped half and half method [26]. The quality of solutions is found by analyzing each tree according to fitness measurement procedure.

In employed bee phase, candidate solution is created using information sharing mechanism which is the most fundamental difference between ABC and ABCP [36]. In this mechanism, when a candidate solution (v_i) is generated, the neighbor node solution x_k, taken from the tree, is randomly selected considering the predetermined probability p_{ip}. The node selected from the neighbor solution x_k determines what information will be shared with the current solution and how much it will be shared. Then node x_i, which represents the current solution in the tree that determines how to use the neighboring node, is randomly selected in the probability distribution of p_{ip}. The candidate solution v_i is produced by replacing

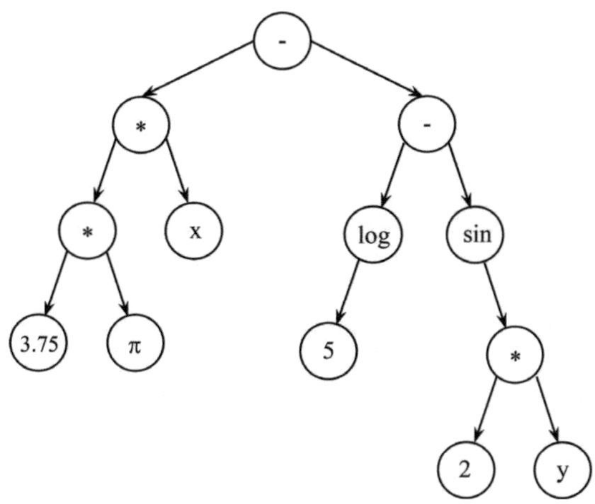

Figure 2.
GP and ABCP solutions are represented by tree structure.

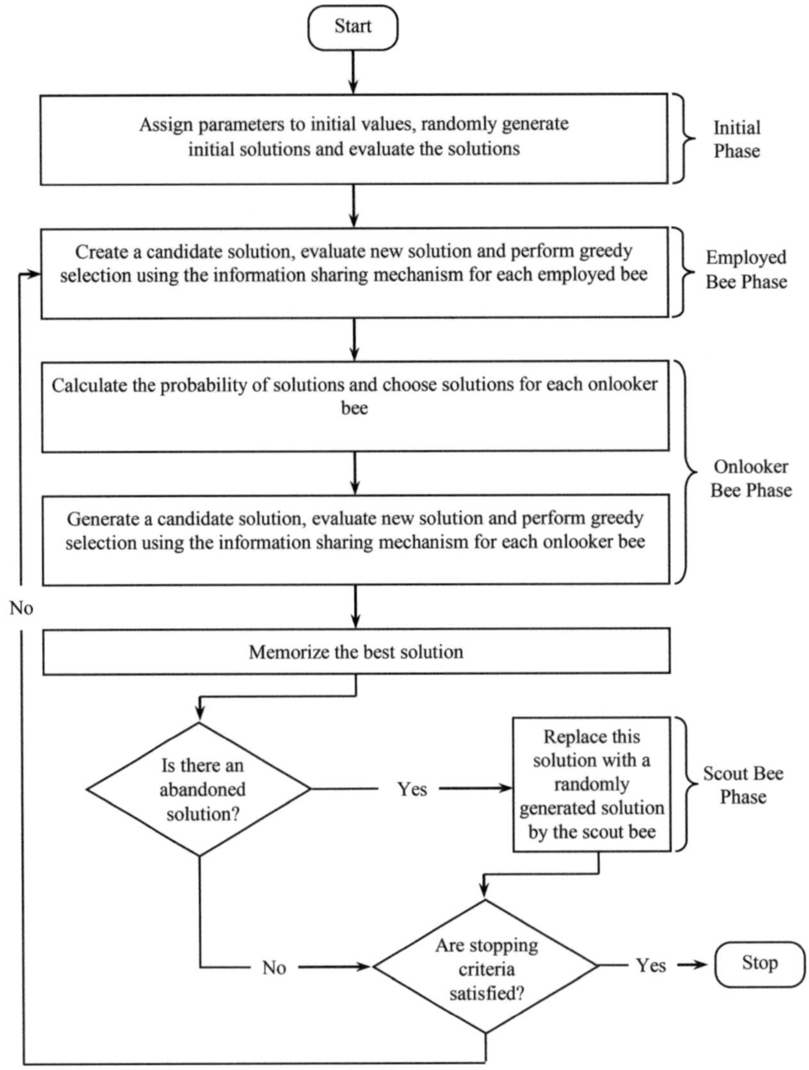

Figure 3.
The flow chart of ABCP.

the nodes of the current solution node x_i and the neighbor solution node x_k. This sharing mechanism is shown in **Figure 4**. **Figure 4a** and **b** are: node x_i representing the current solution and neighbor node x_k taken from the tree respectively, **Figure 4c** neighboring information and the generated candidate solution are given in **Figure 4d**. After the candidate solution is generated, a greedy selection process is applied between the node x_i expressing the current solution and the candidate solution v_i. Candidate solution is evaluated and greedy selection is used for each employed bee.

In onlooker bee phase, employed bees come into hive and share their nectar with the onlooker bees after they complete the research process. The source selection is based on the selection probability of the solution that is based on the nectar qualities, p_i is calculated Eq. (2):

$$p_i = \frac{0.9 * fit_i}{fit_{best}} + 0.1 \qquad (2)$$

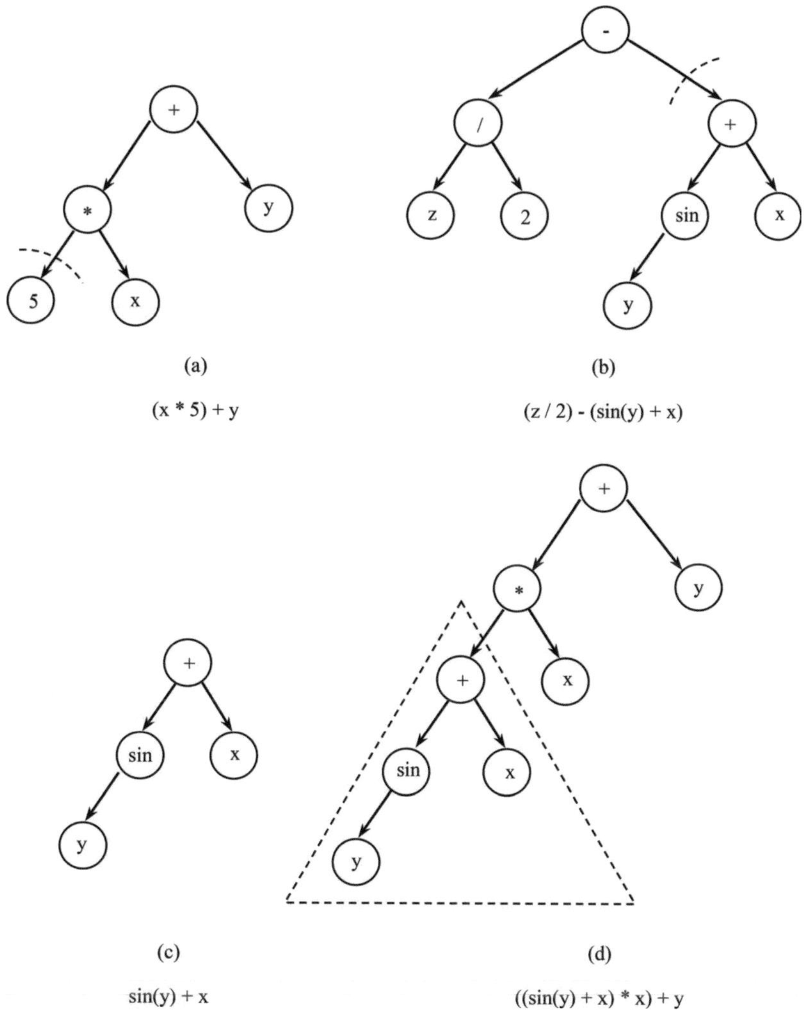

Figure 4.
Example of information sharing mechanism in ABCP.

where fit_i quality of the solution i, fit_{best} quality of the best solution current solutions [35]. When the solutions are selected, the onlooker bees begin to look for new sources by acting like employed bees. The quality of the newly found solution is checked. If a new solution is more qualified, the solution is taken into memory and the current source is deleted from the memory.

After the employed bees and onlooker bees complete the search in each cycle, the penalty points of the respective sources are incremented by one if they cannot find more qualify sources. When a better source is found, the penalty point of that source is reset. If the penalty point exceeds the 'limit' parameter, the employed bee of that source becomes a scout bee and randomly determines new source instead of an abandoned source.

4. Experimental design

This section demonstrate feature selected classification ability of GP and ABCP, set of experiments conducted.

4.1 Datasets

In this chapter, the experiments are conducted on four real world datasets. All datasets are taken from UCI [37]. The first of data set is Wisconsin diagnostic breast cancer (WDBC). The dataset classifies a tumor as either benign or malignant is the diagnosis of breast cancer. It consists of 30 input parameters that determine whether the tumor of 569 patients is benign or malignant. When the data set is examined, it is observed that ~60% of the benign and remainder of the tumors is malignant. The malignant tumor in the data set is defined as 1 and benign tumor is 0. The entry set contains 10 parameters for the suspected community. These input parameters are given as radius, texture, circumference, area, fluency, density, concavity, concavity points, symmetry and fractal. Dataset has an average, standard error, and worst error value for each record. Thus, there are totally 30 input parameters.

It has been used in much recent work on cancer classification of machine learning algorithms [38–40]. Bagui et al. tried to classify two large breast cancer data sets with many machine learning methods such as linear, quadratic, k-NN [39]. In the paper, 9 variable WBC (Wisconsin breast cancer) and 30 variable WDBC (Wisconsin diagnostics breast cancer) data sets were reduced to 6 and 7 variables, respectively. WDBC is classified J48 decision trees, multi-layer perception (MLP), naive Bayes (NB), sequential minimal optimization (SMO), distance based K nearest neighbor (IBK, instance based for K-nearest neighbor) in [40]. Kathija et al. used support vector machines (SVM) and Naive Bayes to classify WDBC in the paper [40].

The second dataset is the dermatology data set, contains 34 features, 33 of which are linear values and one of which is nominal. The differential diagnosis of erythematosquamous disease is a real problem in dermatology. Diagnosis usually requires a biopsy, but unfortunately, these diseases share many histopathological features. Patients were initially evaluated clinically in the data set. Then, skin samples were taken for evaluation of 22 histopathological features. The values of the histopathological features were determined by analysis of the samples under a microscope. There are multiple researches to diagnose dermatological diseases [41–46]. Rambhajani et al. used the Bayesian technique as a feature selection in the paper [42]. When several measures such as accuracy, sensitivity, and specificity are evaluated high successful results obtained in the model classification of 15 features for the dermatology data set with 34 features. Pappa et al. proposed a multi object GA called C4.5 that performed on six different data sets including the dermatology dataset for feature selection [46].

The other dataset is Wine which is the results of chemical analyzes of wines from three different varieties of the same region of Italy. The analysis is based on the amounts of 13 features present in each of the three wine varieties. Zhong et al. proposed a modified approach to the nonsmooth Newton method and compared with support vector algorithm called standard v-KSVCR method in wine dataset [47]. A proposed block based affine matrix for spectral clustering methods was compared with 10 different datasets including wine dataset standard classification methods in [48].

The last dataset Horse colic which reveals the presence or absence of colic disease depending on various pathological values of horse colic. Nock et al. used the symmetric nearest neighbor (SRN), which calculates the scores of the closest neighbor's relations in [49].

This chapter aims to be able to diagnose that the tumor is benign or malignant in WDBC, to identify six different dermatologic diseases in Dermatology, to recognize three varieties of wines in Wine and to presence of colic disease was investigated in Horse Colic.

4.2 Training sets and test sets

In this chapter, each dataset is split into a training set and test set to investigate feature selected classification performance of the evolved models. The number of features, training instances and test instances of the four datasets are shown in **Table 1**. All datasets are almost split with 70% of instances randomly selected from the datasets for training and the other 30% instances forms test set. In each run, the training and test instances are reconstructed by selecting from random instances of datasets.

4.3 Settings

Similar parameter values and functions are used for comparison with GP and ABCP. Since the real input features of the data sets were used, the results obtained from the solutions are theoretically in the range of $[-\infty, \infty]$. Result values to be able to define discrete class values (such as class 0, class 1), it is necessary to be first drawn to a range defined earlier and be contained the total number of classes. The fitness function is defined in Eq. (3).

$$(N_c - 1) * \left(\frac{1}{(1 + \exp(-g_0))} \right) \tag{3}$$

where N_c is the number of output classes, g_o is the result of the current solution. For example, for a problem of class 4, the output of Eq. (3) is in the range [0–3]. The real features found are rounded to the nearest integer value and the solution class features are predicted as '0', '1', '2', '3' in this case.

In this chapter, the fitness function is the weighted sum of the ratios of the total class numbers in the data set of correctly predicted class numbers. For example, in the binary classification, the fitness function is obtained by summing up ratio of correct predicted 0 to total number of 0 in the data set with ratio of correct predicted 1 to total number of 1 in the data set.

For binary classification problems, this function is defined as SFF (sensitivity fitness function) given in Eq. (4) [50].

$$SFF = w\frac{n_c(i,0)}{n_a(i,0)} + (1-w)\frac{n_c(i,1)}{n_a(i,1)} \tag{4}$$

Dataset	Features	Total instances	Training instances	Test instances	Output classes
WDBC	30	569	427	142	2
Dermatology	34	366	274	92	6
Wine	13	178	133	45	3
Horse colic	26	364	273	91	3

Table 1.
Characteristics of the datasets considered in the experiments.

where $n_c(i,k)$ is the number of correctly predicted states when compared to the k class in data set from the class k for the ith solution, $n_a(i,k)$ the number of all records in class k in the data set is the number of inputs defined in the range [0, 1] refers to a real number. The generalized version of Eq. (4) is given in Eq. (5) for multiple class problems investigated.

$$SFF_n = \sum_{j=0}^{n-1} w \frac{n_c(i,j)}{n_a(i,j)} \tag{5}$$

In general, the weight value (w) is used equally. In this case, the proportion of the ratio distribution for each class is adjusted equally. In some cases, a penalty parameter can be added to avoid misclassification in unbalanced data sets. The parameter is added to the fitness function that defined in Eq. (5) as expressed in Eq. (6). It evaluates the models obtained from the solutions. Where p is the penalty factor and N is the total number of nodes in the solution.

$$SFF_n = \sum_{j=0}^{n-1} w \frac{n_c(i,j)}{n_a(i,j)} - pN \tag{6}$$

The data sets are evaluated according to the SFF function defined in Eq. (6). The complexity of the obtained solution is calculated as in Eq. (7) in proportion to the depth of the tree and the number of nodes.

$$C = \sum_{k=1}^{d} n * k \tag{7}$$

where C is tree complexity, d is the depth of the solution tree, and n is the number of nodes at depth.

The control parameters used by the automatic programming methods are given in **Table 2**. The population size and the iteration size are set by the number of features and the number of classes of the data set. Dermatology has more features and classes than other datasets, therefore population size and iteration number are

	WDBC		Dermatology		Wine		Horse colic	
Control parameters	**GP**	**ABCP**	**GP**	**ABCP**	**GP**	**ABCP**	**GP**	**ABCP**
Population/colony size	200	200	300	300	300	300	300	300
Iteration size	150	150	250	250	150	150	250	250
Maximum tree depth	12	12	12	12	12	12	12	12
Tournament size	6	—	6	—	6	—	6	—
Mutation ratio	0.1	—	0.1	—	0.1	—	0.1	—
Crossover ratio	0.8	—	0.8	—	0.8	—	0.8	—
Direct reproduction ratio	0.1	—	0.1	—	0.1	—	0.1	—
w	1/2		1/6		1/3		1/3	
p	0.001		0.001		0.001		0.001	
Functions	+, −, *, tan, sin, cos, square, maxx, minx, exp., ifbte, iflte							

Table 2.
Control parameters of GP and ABCP in the experiments.

chosen as the highest for this dataset. As seen from **Table 2**, the weight value is defined in proportion to the number of classes in the output of each data set. Each class is equal importance. The penalty point given in Eq. (6) was set equal to 0.001 for all data sets. The *maxx* function specifies the maximum value of vector, the *minx* function specifies the minimum value of vector. The *ifbte* checks the value of left operand, if it is greater than or equal to the value of right operand, then condition becomes true. The *iflte* checks the value of left operand, if it is less than or equal to the value of right operand, then condition becomes true. How the functions operate condition expressions are defined in Eqs. (8) and (9).

$$\begin{aligned} &X = ifbte(A, B, C, D) \\ &if(A \geq B)\ then\ \ X = C\ else\ X = d \end{aligned} \tag{8}$$

$$\begin{aligned} &X = iflte(A, B, C, D) \\ &if(A < B)\ then\ \ X = C\ else\ X = d \end{aligned} \tag{9}$$

4.4 Simulation results

For each data set, GP and ABCP are run 30 times according to configuration in **Table 2**. The classification success of GP and ABCP methods are given in **Table 3** in terms of mean, best and worst values for each dataset. SFF and success percentage (SP) results are given in **Table 3** for both training and test cases. As the SFF increased, the success rate of classification increased. The highest mean classification in training (93.43%) was obtained ABCP in Wine. Both methods showed lower SFF and classification success compared to other data sets in Horse colic. The best

		GP				ABCP			
Dataset	**Metrics**	**Train**		**Test**		**Train**		**Test**	
		SFF	**SP**	**SFF**	**SP**	**SFF**	**SP**	**SFF**	**SP**
WDBC	Mean	0.91	92.33	0.9	91.01	0.92	93.27	0.9	91.48
	Standard deviation	0.02	2.56	0.03	3.8	0.02	2.01	0.03	3.07
	Best	0.94	95.32	0.94	95.77	0.95	96.25	0.96	97.89
	Worst	0.86	86.42	0.81	77.46	0.87	87.82	0.84	84.51
Dermatology	Mean	0.81	81.96	0.77	78.66	0.89	92.27	0.85	89.17
	Standard deviation	0.1	15	0.11	13.96	0.02	1.93	0.05	4.4
	Best	0.92	95.26	0.94	96.74	0.93	97.08	0.97	98.91
	Worst	0.6	48.54	0.48	46.74	0.84	89.42	0.77	80.43
Wine	Mean	0.88	88.7	0.85	84.9	0.92	93.43	0.88	88.22
	Standard deviation	0.06	5.94	0.07	7.59	0.02	2.59	0.05	6.83
	Best	0.95	98.5	0.98	100	0.97	98.5	0.98	100
	Worst	0.76	76.69	0.71	73.33	0.88	88.72	0.78	73.33
Horse colic	Mean	0.62	58.81	0.49	50.4	0.67	62.52	0.54	54.76
	Standard deviation	0.06	5.42	0.09	8.35	0.03	3.53	0.07	4.92
	Best	0.71	67.4	0.65	71.43	0.73	69.96	0.65	61.54
	Worst	0.51	47.99	0.3	38.46	0.62	56.78	0.36	45.05

Table 3.
Classification results for each data set.

Dataset	Method	Model of best of run individual	Number of features
WDBC	ABCP	$\cos(x_8 * x_{22}) + \min(x_5, \cos(x_5 * x_{21}))$	4
	GP	$\cos(\mathit{iflte}(\tan(0.7604 * x_{27} * x_{28} * x_{24}), \tan(x_{14}), \tan(0.7390), \cos(x_{17})))$	5
Dermatology	ABCP	$(\mathit{ifbte}(\tan(x_{15}, x_6, (((\tan(\mathit{ifbte}(x_{22}, x_{22}, (\mathit{ifbte}(x_{33}, x_{31}, x_{31}, \mathit{ifbte}(x_{23}, x_{31}, \tan(-2.161), x_{15})) - x_{31}, x_{15}))) - x_{22}) + (\tan(x_5 * x_{34}))), (2x_7 - x_{20})) - x_{22})$	11
	GP	$\mathit{ifbte}(x_{13}, x_{20}, \mathit{ifbte}(x_{13}, x_{27}, \cos(\exp(\mathit{ifbte}(x_{23}, x_5, \cos(x_{15}), x_{31}), x_{23}), (x_{13} - x_{23})))) + (x_{31} - (x_{22} * \exp(x_{22})))$	8
Wine	ABCP	$\mathit{ifbte}(-2.452, (\exp(x_{12}) - x_{10}), 7.5519, ((-2.452 * x_{10}) * \cos(x_7)) * \min(\cos(\cos(x_{10} - x_7)) - x_{13}))))$	4
	GP	$\min(\exp(\sin(x_1), \min(\exp(\cos(x_7)), \cos(\mathit{iflte}(x_9, x_7, \mathit{iflte}(\cos(\exp(\sin(x_1))), \mathit{iflte}(\cos(x_7), x_8, x_7, x_8))x_7,)x_{11})), \tan(\mathit{iflte}(x_{11}, \sin(x_1), x_8, x_7)))$	4
Horse colic	ABCP	$(\mathit{ifbte}(\mathit{square}(\cos(x_{10} + x_{24})), \sin(x_{22}), \mathrm{minx}(x_8, x_{12}) - 4.1591, \sin(\mathit{ifbte}(x_{19}, \exp(\exp(\mathit{iflte}(x_{23}, x_{22}, x_{22}, \sin(x_{22})))), \tan(x_{23}) - x_{22}, x_{22}))))$	7
	GP	$\min(x_6, x_{21}) - \mathit{square}(\min(\mathit{iflte}(x_{22}, x_{10}, \mathit{iflte}(\mathit{square}(x_1), x_{10}, \tan(-6.653), x_1), x_{26}), \min(x_{14}, x_{21})) - \mathit{square}(\min(\mathit{iflte}(\mathit{square}(x_{14}), \mathit{square}(x_8), \tan(x_{23}), -6.655), (x_{23} - x_1))))))$	8

Table 4.
Models of best run ABCP and GP.

models of GP and ABCP have 100% test classification success in Wine. For the case study investigated, compact classification models are obtained with comparable accuracy to GP.

Problem	GP			ABCP		
	Total number of nodes	Depth of the best solution tree	Best solution tree complexity	Total number of nodes	Depth of the best solution tree	Best solution tree complexity
WDBC	16	7	67	**11**	**5**	**36**
Dermatology	**25**	**8**	**107**	37	12	249
Wine	32	9	177	**21**	**7**	**81**
Horse colic	34	9	197	**33**	**9**	**163**

Table 5.
Best solution tree information for each data set.

Program	Metrics	Mean	Standard deviation	Most common features	Features in both GP and ABCP	Number most common features	Number features both GP and ABCP
WDBC	ABCP	4.13	1.33	$x_{28}(15), x_7(12), x_8(11), x_5(7)$	$x_{28}(15), x_7(12), x_8(11)$	4	3
	GP	3.13	1.36	$x_8(12), x_7(12), x_{27}(11), x_{28}(8)$	$x_8(12), x_7(12), x_{28}(8)$	4	3
Dermatology	ABCP	7.20	1.90	$x_{31}(30), x_{15}(29), x_{22}(25), x_{14}(23), x_{33}(15), x_7(12), x_{27}(10), x_6(9)$	$x_{31}(30), x_{15}(29), x_{22}(25), x_{14}(23), x_{33}(15), x_7(12), x_{27}(10)$	8	7
	GP	6.23	1.74	$x_{31}(23), x_{22}(15), x_{14}(15), x_7(13), x_5(10), x_{20}(10), x_{27}(9), x_{15}(9), x_{30}(8), x_{33}(8)$	$x_{31}(23), x_{22}(15), x_{14}(15), x_7(13), x_{27}(9), x_{15}(9), x_{33}(8)$	10	7
Wine	ABCP	4.07	1.18	$x_7(30), x_{11}(26), x_{10}(19), x_{12}(17)$	$x_7(30), x_{11}(26), x_{10}(19), x_{12}(17)$	4	4
	GP	3.17	1.58	$x_7(29), x_{10}(14), x_{12}(12), x_{11}(12)$	$x_7(29), x_{10}(14), x_{12}(12), x_{11}(12)$	4	4
Horse colic	ABCP	6.93	1.41	$x_{23}(27), x_{19}(25), x_{22}(23), x_1(21), x_{21}(13), x_{26}(13), x_8(13), x_{15}(7), x_{10}(7)$	$x_{23}(27), x_{19}(25), x_{22}(23), x_1(21), x_{21}(13), x_{26}(13), x_8(13), x_{10}(7)$	9	8
	GP	5.97	2.36	$x_{23}(15), x_1(15), x_{21}(14), x_{26}(14), x_{19}(14), x_8(13), x_{22}(12), x_7(11), x_{14}(9), x_{10}(9), x_2(7)$	$x_{23}(15), x_1(15), x_{21}(14), x_{26}(14), x_{19}(14), x_8(13), x_{22}(12), x_{10}(9)$	11	8

Table 6.
Number of features selected by the methods.

4.5 Analysis of evolved models

The evolved models of best classifier solutions in ABCP are shown in **Table 4**. It can be observed that both methods extracted successful models with few features. The methods extracted models regardless of the total number of features of the data sets. In general, ABCP has achieved higher success rate of classification than GP using less features.

Table 5 shows general information about the best solution tree. Less complex models are shown in the table with bold typing. When the trees of the best models are analyzed structurally, ABCP, except for the dermatology, shows the best models with less complexity. The detailed information about the inputs of mathematical models of the best solutions in each run are presented in **Table 6**. Features are ordered most common in equations on the table. Equations which are most common, three features (x_7, x_8, x_{28}) are same in WDBC; seven features (x_7, x_{14}, x_{15}, x_{22}, x_{27}, x_{31}, x_{33}) are same in dermatology; four features (x_7, x_{10}, x_{11}, x_{12}) are same in wine; eight features (x_1, x_8, x_{10}, x_{19}, x_{21}, x_{22}, x_{23}, x_{26}) are same in horse colic in both methods. In the best models of the 30 runs, the frequently available features in both of the methods were evaluated as inputs for success of classification. For example, in total 30 runs for WDBC x_{28} 15 times; for dermatology x_{31} were seen.

5. Conclusion

In this chapter, selecting features in classification problems are investigated using GP and ABCP and the literature study related to this field is included. In the performance analysis of the methods, four classification problems are used. As results of 30 runs, the features of the best models were examined. Both methods were found to extract successful models with the same features. According to the experimental results, ABCP is able to extract successful models in training set and it has comparable accuracy to GP. This chapter shows that ABCP can be used in high level automatic programming for machine learning. Several interesting automatic programming methods such as Multi-Gen GP and Multi-Hive ABCP can be further researched in the near future.

Author details

Sibel Arslan and Celal Ozturk*
Computer Engineering Department, Engineering Faculty, Erciyes University, Kayseri, Turkey

*Address all correspondence to: celal@erciyes.edu.tr

References

[1] Nag K, Pal NR. A multiobjective genetic programming based ensemble for simultaneous feature selection and classification. IEEE Transactions on Cybernetics. 2016;**46**:499-510. DOI: 10.1109/TCYB.2015.2404806

[2] Yu J, Yu J, Almal AA, Dhanasekaran SM, Ghosh D, Worzel WP, et al. Feature selection and molecular classification of cancer using genetic programming. Neoplasia. 2007;**9**(4):292-303. DOI: 10.1593/neo.07121

[3] Zhang Y, Rockett PI. Domain-independent feature extraction for multi-classification using multi-objective genetic programming. Pattern Analysis and Applications. 2010;**13**(3): 273-288. DOI: 10.1007/s10044-009-0154-1

[4] Muni DP, Pal NR, Das J. Genetic programming for simultaneous feature selection and classifier design. IEEE Transactions on Systems, Man, and Cybernetics. 2006;**36**(1):106-117. DOI: 10.1109/TSMCB.2005.854499

[5] Cai R, Hao Z, Yang X, Wen W. An efficient gene selection algorithm based on mutual information. Neurocomputing. 2009;**72**:91-999. DOI: 10.1016/j.neucom.2008.04.005

[6] Saeys Y, Inza I, Larranaga P. Review of feature selection techniques in bioinformatics. Bioinformatics. 2007; **23**(19):2507-2517. DOI: 10.1093/bioinformatics/btm344

[7] Xue B, Zhang M, Browne WN, Yao X. A survey on evolutionary computation approaches to feature selection. IEEE Transactions on Evolutionary Computation. 2016;**20**(4): 606-626. DOI: 10.1109/TEVC.2015.2504420

[8] Guyon I, Elisseeff A. An introduction to variable and feature selection. Journal of Machine Learning Research. 2003;**3**: 1157-1182

[9] Gulgezen G. Kararlı ve başarımı yüksek öznitelik seçimi. Istanbul Technical University; 2009

[10] Zhang Y, Wanga S, Phillips P, Ji G. Binary PSO with mutation operator for feature selection using decision tree applied to spam detection. Knowledge-Based Systems. 2014;**64**:22-31. DOI: 10.1016/j.knosys.2014.03.015

[11] Sikora R, Piramuthu S. Framework for efficient feature selection in genetic algorithm based data mining. European Journal of Operational Research. 2007; **180**:723-737. DOI: 10.1016/j.ejor.2006.02.040

[12] Dy JG, Brodley CE. Feature selection for unsupervised learning. Journal of Machine Learning Research. 2004;**5**: 845-889

[13] Schiezaro M, Pedrini H. Data feature selection based on artificial bee colony algorithm. EURASIP Journal on Image and Video Processing. 2013;**47**:1-8

[14] Landry JA, Costa LD, Bernier T. Discriminant feature selection by genetic programming: Towards a domain independent multiclass object detection system. Systemics Cybernetics and Informatics. 2006;**3**(1):7681

[15] Fidelis MV, Lopes HS, Freitas AA. Discovering comprehensible classification rules with a genetic algorithm. In: IEEE, Proceedings of the Congress; Vol. 1. 2000. pp. 805-810. DOI: 10.1109/CEC.2000.870381

[16] Athitsos V, Sclaroff S. Boosting nearest neighbor classifiers for multiclass recognition. In: Computer Science Tech Report; 2004. DOI: 10.1109/CVPR.2005.424

[17] Venkatesan R, Er MJ. A novel progressive learning technique for multiclass classification. Neurocomputing. 2016;**207**:310-321. DOI: 10.1016/j.neucom.2016.05.006

[18] Awuley A, Ross BJ. Feature selection and classification using age layered population structure genetic programming. In: CEC 2016; 2016. DOI: 10.1109/CEC.2016.7744088

[19] Lin JY, Ke HR, Chien BC, Yang WP. Classifier design with feature selection and feature extraction using layered genetic programming. Expert Systems with Applications. 2008;**34**(2): 1384-1393. DOI: 10.1016/j.eswa.2007.01.006

[20] Ahmed S, Zhang M, Peng L. Feature selection and classification of high dimensional mass spectrometry data, a genetic programming approach. In: Evolutionary Computation, Machine Learning and Data Mining in Bioinformatics. 11th European Conference EvoBIO 2013. Vienna, Austria; 2013. pp. 43-55. DOI: 10.1007/978-3-642-37189-9_5

[21] Liu KH, Tong M, Xie ST, Yee VT. Genetic programming based ensemble system for microarray data classification. Computational and Mathematical Methods in Medicine. Hindawi Publishing Corporation. 2015; **2**:1-11. DOI: 10.1155/2015/193406

[22] Karaboga D, Ozturk C. A novel clustering approach: Artificial bee colony (ABC) algorithm. Applied Soft Computing. 2011;**11**:652-657. DOI: 10.1016/j.asoc.2009.12.025

[23] Karaboga D, Ozturk C. Neural networks training by artificial bee colony algorithm on pattern classification. Neural Network World: International Journal on Neural and Mass Parallel Computing and Information Systems. 2009;**19**(3): 279-292

[24] Joyanth J, Kumar A, Koliwad S, Krishnashastry S. Artificial bee colony algorithm for classification of remote sensed data. In: Industrial Instrumentation and Control (ICIC), International Conference. 2015. DOI: 10.1109/IIC.2015.7150989

[25] Chung YY, Yeh W, Wahid N, Mujahid A, Zaidi A. Artificial bee colony based data mining algorithms for classification tasks. Modern Applied Science. 2011;**5**(4):217-231. DOI: 10.5539/mas.v5n4p217

[26] Koza J. Genetic Programming: On the Programming of Computers by Means of Natural Selection. Cambridge, MA, USA: MIT Press; 1992

[27] Koza J. Genetic Programming II: Automatic Discovery of Reusable Programs. Cambridge, MA: MIT Press; 1994

[28] Koza J, Bennett F, Andre D, Keane M. Genetic Programming III: Darwinian Invention and Problem Solving. IEEE Transactions on Evolutionary Computation. San Francisco, CA; **3**(3):251-253

[29] Zhang L, Nandi AK. Fault classification using genetic programming. Mechanical Systems and Signal Processing. 2007;**21**(3): 1273-1284. DOI: 10.1016/j.ymssp.2006.04.004

[30] Settea S, Boullartb L. Genetic programming: Principles and applications. Engineering Applications of Artificial Intelligence. 2001;**14**:727-736. DOI: 10.1016/S0952-1976(02)00013-1

[31] Poli R, Langdon W, McPhee N. A Field Guide to Genetic Programming. England, UK; 2008:19-27. http://lulu.com, Creative Commons Attribution, Noncommercial-No Derivative Works 2.0

[32] Gan Z, Chow TWS, Chau WN. Clone selection programming and its

application to symbolic regression. Expert Systems with Applications. 2009;**36**:3996-4005. DOI: 10.1016/j.eswa.2008.02.030

[33] Karaboga D. Yapay Zeka Optimizasyon Algoritmaları. Nobel Yayınları; 2011

[34] Karaboga D. An Idea Based On Honey Bee Swarm for Numerical Optimization. Technical Report TR06. Erciyes University, Engineering Faculty, Computer Engineering Department; 2005

[35] Karaboga D, Ozturk C, Karaboga N, Gorkemli B. Artificial bee colony programming for symbolic regression. Information Sciences. 2012;**209**:115. DOI: 10.1016/j.ins.2012.05.002

[36] Gorkemli B. Yapay Arı Koloni Programlama (ABCP) yöntemlerinin geliştirilmesi ve sembolik regresyon problemlerine uygulanması, PhD Thesis, Erciyes University, Engineering Faculty, Computer Engineering Department; 2015

[37] UC Irvine Machine Learning Repository. [Online]. Available from: http://archive.ics.uci.edu/ml/index.php

[38] Bagui S, Bagui S, Hemasinha R. The statistical classification of breast cancer data. International Journal of Statistics and Applications. 2016;**6**(1):15-22. DOI: 10.5923/j.statistics.20160601.03

[39] Salama GI, Abdelhalim MB, Zeid MA. Breast cancer diagnosis on three different datasets using multiclassifiers. International Journal of Computer and Information Technology. 2012;**01**:2277-0764

[40] Kathija A, Nisha S. Breast cancer data classification using SVM and naive Bayes techniques. International Journal of Innovative Research in Computer and Communication Engineering. 2016;**4**:12

[41] Guvenir HA, Demiröz G, Ilter N. Learning differential diagnosis of erythematosquamous diseases using voting feature intervals. Artificial Intelligence in Medicine. 1998;**13**: 147-165

[42] Rambhajani M, Deepanker W, Pathak N. Classification of dermatology diseases through Bayes net and best first search. International Journal of Advanced Research in Computer and Communication Engineering. 2015;**4**(5): 116-119. DOI: 10.17148/IJARCCE.2015.4526

[43] Manjusha K, Sankaranarayanan K, Seena P. Data mining in dermatological diagnosis: A method for severity prediction. International Journal of Computers and Applications. 2015; **117**(11):0975-8887

[44] Barati E, Saraee M, Mohammadi A, Adibi N, Ahamadzadeh MR. A survey on utilization of data mining approaches for dermatological (skin) diseases prediction. Cyber Journals: Multidisciplinary Journals in Science and Technology. Journal of Selected Areas in Health Informatics (JSHI). March Edition, 2011:1-11

[45] Parikh KS, Shah TP, Kota R, Vora R. Diagnosing common skin diseases using soft computing techniques. International Journal of Bio-Science and Bio-Technology. 2015;7(6):275-286. DOI: 10.1109/ICASTECH.2009.5409725

[46] Pappa GL, Freitas AA, Kaestner CAA. Attribute selection with a multi objective genetic algorithm. In: SBIA; 2002

[47] Zhong P, Fukushima M. A regularized non-smooth newton method for multiclass support vector machines. Optimization Methods and Software. 2007;**22**:225-236. DOI: 10.1080/10556780600834745

[48] Fischer I, Poland J. Amplifying the block matrix structure for spectral

clustering. Technical Report No. IDSIA0305; 2005

[49] Nock R, Sebban M, Bernard D. A simple locally adaptive nearest neighbor rule with application to pollution forecasting. International Journal of Pattern Recognition and Artificial Intelligence. 2003;**17**(8):1369-1382. DOI: 10.1142/S0218001403002952

[50] Morrison GA, Searson DP, Willis MJ. Using genetic programming to evolve a team of data classifiers. International Journal of Computer, Electrical, Automation, Control and Information Engineering. 2010;**4**(72): 261-264

Chapter 5

Sensor-Driven, Spatially Explicit Agent-Based Models

Francis Oloo

Abstract

Conventionally, agent-based models (ABMs) are specified from well-established theory about the systems under investigation. For such models, data is only introduced to ensure the validity of the specified models. In cases where the underlying mechanisms of the system of interest are unknown, rich datasets about the system can reveal patterns and processes of the systems. Sensors have become ubiquitous allowing researchers to capture precise characteristics of entities in both time and space. The combination of data from in situ sensors to geospatial outputs provides a rich resource for characterising geospatial environments and entities on earth. More importantly, the sensor data can capture behaviours and interactions of entities allowing us to visualise emerging patterns from the interactions. However, there is a paucity of standardised methods for the integration of dynamic sensor data streams into ABMs. Further, only few models have attempted to incorporate spatial and temporal data dynamically from sensors for model specification, calibration and validation. This chapter documents the state of the art of methods for bridging the gap between sensor data observations and specification of accurate spatially explicit agent-based models. In addition, this work proposes a conceptual framework for dynamic validation of sensor-driven spatial ABMs to address the risk of model overfitting.

Keywords: data-driven models, sensor-driven models, dynamic spatial models, spatial simulation models

1. Introduction

Agent-based models (ABMs) are mathematical models that attempt to reveal system-level properties by representing local-level behaviour and interaction of entities that make up the system [1]. Agents include people, animals, robots, vehicles, plants and smart devices that may be linked in a network, etc. ABMs have been applied to investigate systems in ecology [2, 3], human behaviour [4], epidemiology [5–7], public transport [8, 9], diffusion of technology [10], land use change [11], industrial processes, economics and psychology, among other areas.

An important characteristic of agent-based models is their ability to reveal the emergence of system-level patterns from the local-level behaviours and interactions of system components [12]. However, one traditional weakness of ABMs is their over-reliance on existing theories about the system of phenomena of interest [13]. Over-reliance on domain knowledge limits the application of ABMs in situations where knowledge about the system of interest is incomplete. In such cases, parameter values and behavioural rulesets have to be assumed, thus reducing the plausibility of the models [14]. In addition, in knowledge-driven models, face validation [15] is preferred to statistical validation. Specifically, modelled system behaviours are compared against the qualitative patterns as described in the theories or in the implicit expert knowledge. Moreover, validation is usually implemented as the final step of model specification, hence hindering the dynamic verification of the models during the simulation runs. In very dynamic systems, the model is thus likely to deviate from the real-world scenario unless data about the dynamics of the real world is incorporated into the model during the simulation process.

Due to the limited computational resources and lack of fine-scaled spatial data, ABMs were historically nonspatial, implying that geographic characteristics of the systems of interest were not explicitly specified in the model [16]. As an example, to understand market dynamics, service area of the market of interest may be specified as a Cartesian grid with random cells representing business entities, while consumers are specified as points that move randomly across the modelling surface. Even though such a model can answer generic questions on the consumer behaviour, it may not be able to provide specific insights of the influence of spatial context on the market dynamics.

Advances in sensor technology have made it possible to collect accurate georeferenced data about entities and systems of interest [17]. Fine-scaled sensor data from remote locations are now available for analysis and visualisation. For instance, spatial entities such as humans, vehicles, buildings, animals and plants can be monitored via sensor data streams, revealing interesting spatial and temporal characteristics of these agents. This rich data can provide behavioural information [18, 19] for specifying accurate data-driven models to study the dynamics of the agents of interest.

The emergence of sensor data has not only heightened the interest in spatial ABMs [20] but has also motivated the specification of data-driven models [21] for accurate environmental monitoring and simulation [22]. At the same time, the dynamic nature of sensor data streams has motivated research to bridge the gap between sensor observations and modelling frameworks as a way of facilitating bidirectional communication between sensor observation networks and environmental monitoring systems.

Unfortunately, the progress in sensor-driven spatial simulation models has been ad hoc, with no standardised methods for incorporating data into spatially explicit models. The existing implementations have aimed to address the needs of various disciplines. For instance, in the sensor community, research in sensor web networks [23] is geared towards improving communication, computation and sensor resource management. On the other hand, in computer science, sensor-based research is geared towards developing methods of pervasive computing [24, 25], artificial intelligence and related areas. Due to the multidisciplinary nature of spatial simulation research, documenting the body of knowledge of sensor-driven simulation modelling is critical for the research community.

Spatial systems are special [26] due to the inherent spatial relationships and temporal characteristics of geographic entities. It is therefore necessary to consider the spatio-temporal context [27, 28] and relationships when modelling and simulating spatial processes. Attempts to introduce data into spatial simulation models must be cognizant of the unique characteristics of the spatial systems. This work synthesises the existing methods for dynamic assimilation of sensor data into spatially explicit ABMs and proposes a potential method to address model overfitting that is common to most data-driven modelling methods.

2. Traditional knowledge-driven models

2.1 Essential building blocks of spatial agent-based models

Patterns are the holy grail of spatial agent-based models [29, 30], implying that reproducing spatial patterns is an important characteristic of spatial agent-based simulation. The three important aspects of spatial systems include agents, spatial context or environment and interactions between agents and their environment.

2.1.1 Spatial agents

Spatial agents include autonomous entities that can be characterised by their geographic attributes. Geographic attributes are critical in linking the agent to a unique spatial location and context of its environment. Distinctive attributes of spatial agents include spatial intelligence and spatial interactions. Spatial intelligence entails awareness of the geographic differences of the environment, hence being able to make autonomous decisions over a geographic space [31]. Moreover, spatial intelligence allows agents to interact with other spatial entities and adapt to spatial realities [32].

In defining the character and behaviour of agents in spatial simulation models, traditional models have ignored empirical data and instead used documented knowledge about the agents or random initialisation of agent characteristics [33]. This raises the question on whether such models are immune to the challenge of path dependence [34] that bedevils most ABMs.

2.1.2 Spatial environment

Initially, the variations in the environment of ABMs were commonly specified as an artificial lattice with random variables [35, 36]. With the improvements in computation, and availability of spatial data in both vector and raster data models, spatial data has been introduced to introduce geographic variability and context the in the environment [37]. In particular, the use of remote sensing products has improved the specification of geographic modelling environments [38].

2.1.3 Spatial interactions

Spatial interaction entails the ability to sense, communicate and respond stimuli from other entities based on their geographic proximity or connections. Interaction is the distinctive attribute of spatial ABMs, differentiating such models from other microsimulation models. Whereas initially there has been little empirical data to reveal the interaction between agents, in situ sensors are now capable of capturing detailed aspects of agent interactions including proximity, avoidance, competition and spatial linkages. For instance, trajectories of birds in navigation have been used to describe the social interactions and leadership strategies that are adopted by birds [39]. Also, physiological sensors have been used to detect emotional reactions of road users in urban traffic [40, 41]. Similarly, there are portable sensors that can be used to monitor the health of human agents remotely [42]. Data from such sensor deployments can improve the specification of agent interactions and contribute to the accuracy of agent-based models.

2.2 Conventional modelling cycle

Traditionally, the modelling cycle [43] begins by building a conceptual model about the real-world system of interest. The conceptual model is created from repeated observations of the mechanisms of the real-world system or by relying on documented knowledge about the system. From observations and the domain knowledge, important entities, interactions and patterns are identified. A hypothesis of how the individual level interactions of the agents lead to the emergence of system-level patterns is then formulated. At this level, the use of empirical data is limited to identifying essential entities, interactions and characteristic patterns of the system of focus (**Figure 1**).

Based on the conceptual model, a formal model specification could be undertaken to test a specific hypothesis. Model specification requires the definition of parameters to guide the operation of the model. The choice of the parameters and essential behaviour models depends on the expertise of the modeller and prevailing knowledge of the system under investigation [44]. This in essence means that different modellers can specify different ABMs to test the same hypothesis. It may so happen that different models can confirm the hypothesis, raising the question on true model for addressing the hypothesis in question.

Empirical data is rarely used during model specification; this is both epistemic and strategic. Epistemic in the sense that rather than starting with the data, a plausible model that is founded on sound knowledge should produce data, which is comparable to empirical data from the real world [45]. In addition, agents interact based on their knowledge of their environment and goals and not so much based on their rigorous analysis of data. The limited use of data in ABMs is also strategic to prevent the contamination of model with empirical data, which may ultimately lead to model overfitting.

Upon a successful model specification, the process of verification confirms the logical consistency between the specified behaviour and the known behaviour of the system. The verified model then becomes a candidate for calibration.

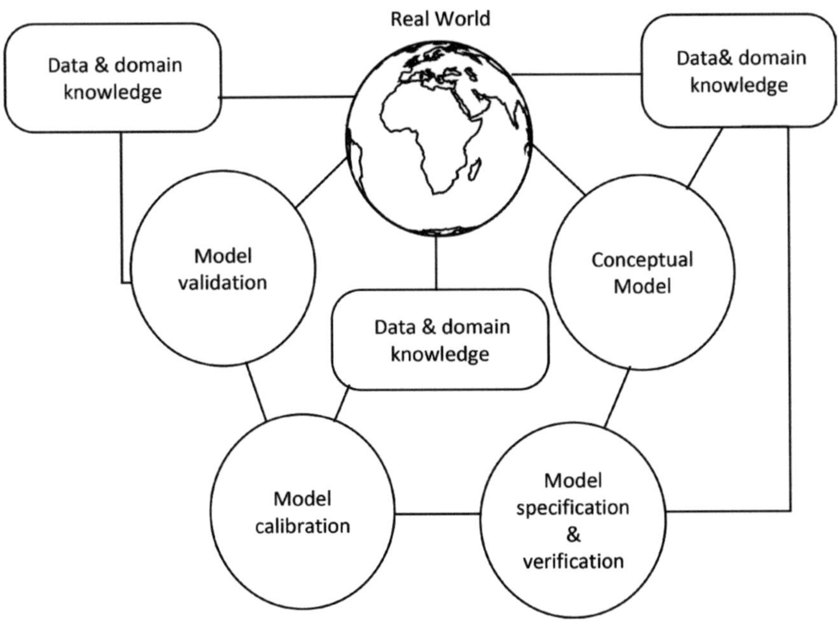

Figure 1.
Application of data and domain knowledge in the conventional modelling life cycle. The cycles represent the important steps in the specification of ABMs. The real world hosts the systems of interest. Observations, expert knowledge and data about the systems in the real world provide the foundational concepts for building the conceptual model. Foundational knowledge and patterns from the real world are used for model specification, calibration and validation. A properly validated model can then be used to test hypothesis and to represent the dynamics of a system in the real world.

The calibration step entails comparing a specified model against empirical data to determine the parameter space for accurate simulation of patterns and dynamics in the real system. A popular method for calibration is the use of pattern-oriented modelling (POM) approach [46]. In POM approach, model calibration involves evaluating parameters based on their ability to replicate multiple patterns that are evident in the real world. In traditional modelling frameworks, historical data may be used in calibration and in other components of the agent-based modelling life cycle.

Validation process is usually the last step in the modelling cycle and involves assessing the degree to which a model is an accurate representation of the real-world system for which it is meant to simulate [47]. For validation, qualitative approaches may be adopted to compare the results from the models against patterns that are observable in the real world. In particular the use of face validation which may include animation or graphical representation is usually the first step in traditional ABM validation [48]. Once again, according to POM framework, an accurate model should be able to produce patterns that are inherent in the real world but which are not explicitly defined in the model.

Apart from qualitative methods, statistical methods [49] may also be adopted to validate the models by comparing the statistical variance between the results of the model against empirical. Statistical comparison is suitable for models that produce detailed quantitative state variables that can be compared to related observations from the real world. A properly specified, rigorously calibrated and accurately validated model can then be deployed for simulation to represent the system of interest and to explore the internal operations of systems of interest.

In summary, the rationale for incorporation of data into traditional agent-based models is to ensure quality and credibility throughout all the modelling stages [50, 51].

2.3 Standards for the specification of ABMs

Because of the straightforward manner of specifying knowledge-driven models, such models are simpler to specify and easy to communicate. The publication of standards to guide ABM specification [52] and protocols like transparent and comprehensive ecological modelling (TRACE) documentation [53], pattern-oriented modelling [46] and Overview, Design Concepts and Details (ODD) protocol [54, 55] have greatly contributed to streamlining the process of model specification. In addition, depending on domain knowledge ensures that models are only acceptable when their results confirm the documented knowledge hence helping to weed out models that result in spurious outcome. The multidisciplinary nature of geographic information science avails knowledge from related disciplines including ecology, computer science, geography, environmental science, economics and psychology, which can support the specification of spatially explicit agent-based models. In the reverse direction, properly specified spatial simulation models can support hypothesis testing and representation of dynamics of systems in other disciplines.

2.4 Critiques of knowledge-driven ABMs

In spite of the benefits of knowledge-driven ABMs, there have been critiques of aspects that limit their broad adoption and application. In particular, the process of model specification depends on the knowledge and expertise of the modeller; as such, discovery of patterns and the specification of behavioural rulesets in the model may be arduous task in situations where the system of interest is not well understood [56]. In addition, the ad hoc manner of model specification may result in multiple models for the same system without bringing clarity on the internal workings of the system. Further, lack of modules to actualise rigorous data mining within the simulation suites has hindered the development of agent-based model that can take advantage of the growing big geospatial data. Moreover, the dependence on domain knowledge and the expertise of individual modellers worsen the gap between modelled examples and the ever-growing data volumes. Individual modellers cannot keep pace with the growth of data, hence necessitating the development of automated methods for model discovery and analysis.

Last but not the least, whereas knowledge-driven models can support the specification of simple models, such models are usually weak in predicting future behaviours of the system [57]. This is more so when the potential effect of various inputs on future states of a system is unknown. As an example, initially, it was possible to model the generic annual behaviour of migratory birds particularly in the wintering months. However, with the reality of human-induced changes to the environment, some birds avoid the long winter journeys and instead find food and warm nesting places around garbage disposal sites in the northern hemisphere [58]. Such specific adaptive behaviours were only detectable through analysis of the empirical trajectories of the birds.

Bridging the gap between the advances in big geospatial sensor data and spatially explicit ABMs requires robust methods for automated pattern detection and model discovery.

2.5 Multi-agent systems and swarm intelligence

Multi-agent systems (MAS) are an extension of single-agent systems and comprise of multiple software agents interacting with each other and their environment to achieve certain goals. Important characteristics of multi-agent systems include communication, collaboration and interaction. In MAS, the agents can either be intelligent or reactive [59]. Intelligent agents are those that are able to logically use knowledge and information at their disposal to make rational decisions. On the other hand, reactive agents respond to the realities of their environment. In multi-agent systems with reactive agents, system-level robustness and complexity emerges from local-level interactions of the constituent agents. Collective intelligence that emerges from MAS is similar to those of swarm intelligence (SI), hence promoting the adoption of MAS in SI [60].

Swarm intelligence has its foundation in the behaviour of natural bio-systems [61]. Specifically, social organisms like bee and ant colonies, flocks of birds and schools of fish have been known to exhibit impressive collective behaviours that may not be directly linked to the capabilities of individual organisms. Swarm intelligence is therefore an attempt to adopt ideas and knowledge from the natural bio-systems to build robust algorithms with application in a number of fields. In particular, in swarm intelligence, software agents are specified to mimic the behaviour of natural systems with the aim of achieving specific goal through the emergence of coherent and functional patterns from the collective behaviour of interacting entities. The particular characteristics of software agents in swarm intelligence include autonomy, interaction, distributed functioning and self-organisation, ensuring that the software agents solve problems at hand without a central control. Swarm intelligence has been employed to build solutions for optimisation, computer network-based search, wireless sensor networks and traffic control, among other areas. Epistemologically, there are two motivations for swarm intelligence [62], the first being to learn about natural system and to understand the emergence of system-level patterns from collective interactions of individual entities of a system. The second motivation is to discover novel algorithms that can be used to solve various engineering, social and computer science problems.

A number of signature algorithms have been developed to actualise swarm intelligence in various applications. The most common of these algorithms include ant colony optimization (ACO), bee colony optimization (BCO) [63] and particle swarm optimization (PSO) [64]. ACO is motivated by the foraging behaviour of ant colonies. Specifically, as individual ants forage for food, they release a chemical known as pheromone when they succeed at finding food. Other members of the colony can detect the pheromone and move to the spot where food has been found. The pheromone evaporates with time. This type of communication between members of a colony ensures an efficient search for food. This model has been applied to simulate swarm intelligence in public transport services [65]. Bee colony optimization algorithms mimic the foraging behaviours of bee colonies where individual bees make characteristic "dances" to alert the members of the colony on the locations of food availability. Other members of the colony can choose to go to this spot by a certain probability. Particle swarm optimization are stochastic optimisation techniques that are inspired by the goal-oriented behaviour of flocking birds [66] that improve the efficiency of their navigation and foraging behaviours through collaboration, cooperation and independent local-level decisions. Particles in a swarm are considered to have limited intelligence and autonomy and exercise simple local-level rules to optimise their flow. PSO has been applied to optimise network-based communication.

Apart from the main algorithms for swarm intelligence, other algorithms which are motivated by natural systems have been tested in multi-agent systems and later adapted for swarm intelligence; these include genetic algorithms, neural networks, re-enforced learning and simulated annealing. Apart from serving as a test bed for nature inspired algorithm, MAS also provide a platform for specifying, modelling and simulating natural systems, thus contributing to the knowledge that is then ultimately adapted in swarm intelligence. The emergence of sophisticated sensors has made it possible to embed sensor in systems of interest. The sensor data can then be used to specify multi-agent models of the system allowing biologists and computer scientists to learn the behaviours of these systems, hence making it possible to simulate these to improve the algorithms for swarm intelligence [67].

3. Foundations of data-driven agent-based models

3.1 Influence of data in the character of agent-based models

There are three broad motivations for specifying agent-based models including testing hypothesis about a particular system, representing the dynamics of a system and predicting the potential future states of a system. Empirical data has traditionally been used in ABMs to characterise agents in the model, for model initialisation and for validation [68]. Injecting data into agent-based models can influence the purpose of the models. Consequently, three general types of agent-based models with distinct roles depending on the degree to which data is used to aide their specification emerge. The three categories include generator models, mediator models and predictive models (**Figure 2**).

3.1.1 Generator models

Generator models are the most common types of agent-based models and have their foundations in generative social sciences [69]. These models rely heavily on the domain knowledge and the expertise of the modellers to specify behaviour rules and model structures. Consequently, such models are predominantly used for

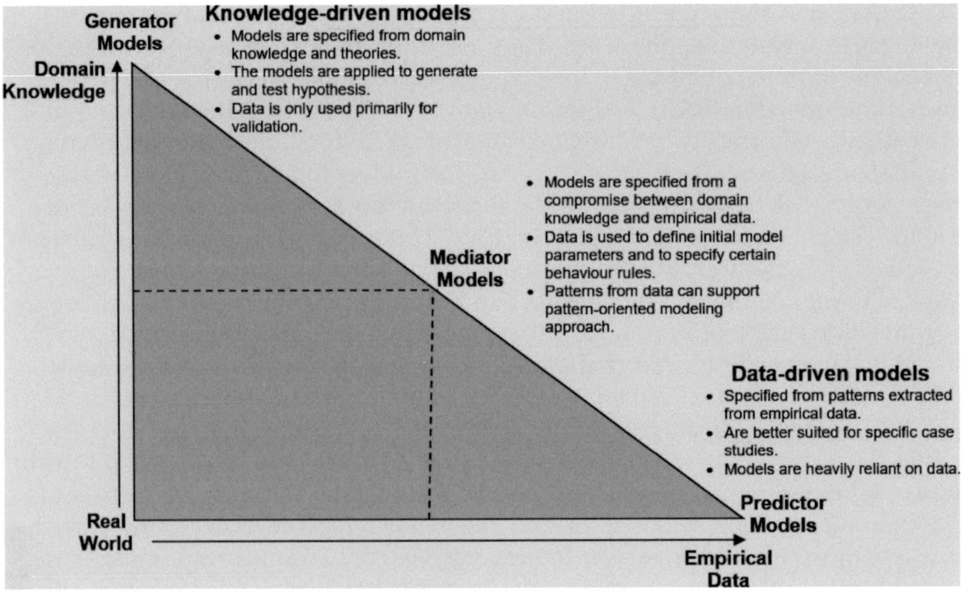

Figure 2.
Categories of agent-based models depending on the degree of data used in the models. Generator models rely heavily on the domain knowledge and are suited for "generating" system scenarios based on variations of input parameters. Mediator model combine both domain knowledge and patterns extracted from data to improve the understanding of a system. Data-driven models are heavily reliant on data and perform better as prediction models.

generating and testing different hypotheses [70]. Generator models aim to demonstrate or "generate" a scenario based on the foundational theories of the dynamic of a system of interest. The models may require minimal data to support initialisation, calibration and validation. By relying on domain knowledge and ingesting marginal data, such models are generic and can replicate related systems. However, the models cannot be relied on to reveal very detailed dynamics of the systems.

3.1.2 Mediator models

The second category of models are the mediator models that move beyond hypothesis testing and attempt to create a better understanding of the system of interest, hence attempting to explain the dynamics of a system. In these models, empirical data provide additional interesting patterns and parameters for model specification. Validation step then confirms whether the models can replicate the patterns that are apparent in the empirical data. Such models can be used to evaluate the implications of empirical research on formal theories [71]. A distinction between mediator models and the generator models is that the modellers do not require complete knowledge about the systems of interest. Specification of accurate models can be achieved by combining partial knowledge of the systems with important characteristics of the system as captured in data. As an example, crowd behaviour in an enclosed building can be studied from video data [72] and used to improve models that represent the behaviour of crowd agents.

3.1.3 Predictor models

Whereas knowledge-driven models can be generic and be applicable to test broad system characteristics, they have not been particularly strong in predicting very specific and detailed aspects in the future system characteristics. In contrast, models that are fuelled by rich datasets are likely to perform better as predictive models [7, 73]. The rich data supports the understanding of the respective system by revealing useful inputs and systemic behaviours that can be used in specifying the model structure [74]. For instance, a fire model that is trained with accurate spatial data on the vegetation characteristics, climatic variables and other contextual information regarding fire dynamics in a particular locality is likely to predict future fire scenarios better than a model that is based on the general understanding of fire dynamics [75].

Domain knowledge provides a good starting point for specifying realistic models for hypothesis testing and for representing behaviours of systems. However, the lack of solid foundational knowledge should not be a handicap for the specification of accurate agent-based models. In an emerging field like geographic information science, the process of knowledge discovery should continue in tandem with the advances in methods that can facilitate infusion of rich data into agent-based models. This can create a mutually beneficial feedback between knowledge-driven models and data-driven model. Importantly, there are concepts in spatial science that are yet to be defined in a crisp manner. The development of data-rich and spatially explicit simulation models can therefore contribute towards building the understanding of some concepts in spatial science, particularly those that concern spatial behaviours [76].

Models that entirely depend on historical knowledge and static datasets may be limited by their failure to appreciate the dynamic conditions of spatio-temporal systems [77] that can only be revealed by capturing the data in near real time. In addition, spatial simulation models which rely primarily on conventional spatial data models may be limited in capturing all the necessary spatial processes [38]. It is therefore important to augment the spatial data models with sensor data streams or other ambient positioning methods that can capture the multiple dimensions of spatial phenomena and processes. Moreover, an understanding of dynamic spatial processes requires the specification of data-driven models that can combine both spatial data models and spatial process models. Sensor data streams can capture dynamic spatial events [78] and associated processes, hence supporting a tighter link between dynamic data and dynamic spatially explicit agent-based models.

3.2 Dynamic data-driven simulation models

In the last two decades, there have been attempts to achieve dynamic data-driven simulation models (DDDABM). This is more so in systems that are characterised by dynamic spatial and temporal behaviours [79]. Advances in sensor capabilities are a major driver of the attempts to actualise dynamic data-driven application systems (DDDAS). In particular, miniaturisation of the sensors, improvement in computational power and developments in telecommunication have led to the growth of robust sensor web networks that can be adopted to address questions in various spatial domains. Importantly, the growth of geosensor networks has made it possible for sensors to capture not only the geographic locations of entities but also the behavioural characteristics of such entities [80, 81]. For example, there are sensors that can capture both the location and multidimensional acceleration of animals, hence revealing their energy use during different activities [82]. The sensor measurements can be related to animal behaviours in different settings, hence allowing for the behaviour of animals to be documented remotely. Another example includes the possibility of capturing location, mobility characteristics and fuel consumption in vehicles, hence linking the mobility patterns to energy use efficiency and safety [83].

Within the wireless sensor networks (WSN), a common approach for actualising dynamic data driven simulation has been to specify sensors as software agents within the model [84]. Such an architecture allows the sensor data to influence the specification of the agent-based model, while the output from the simulation influences the sensor measurement strategies and network configuration. Moreover, agent-based specification of sensor nodes allows for optimisation of the network resources and promotes energy efficiency within the WSN [85]. The bidirectional feedback between wireless sensor networks and the software agents is mutually beneficial both for the efficiency of sensor data collection and for the accuracy of the simulation models. There are three general approaches for actualising data-driven agent-based simulation. These include decoupled data integration, dynamic unidirectional data integration and dynamic bidirectional data assimilation.

3.2.1 Decoupled data integration

In this first approach, data is decoupled from the simulation and is only introduced sparingly to influence various steps in the modelling workflow. For instance, data may be used in specifying the initial conditions of agents, defining the initial model parameters, supporting calibration and validation of spatial agent-based models [56]. For this kind of approach, archival data in the form of surveys [13] or historical movement trajectories of agents may be adopted. The data provides the main characteristics of the agents and possibly also the transition probabilities from one state to the next. However, since such models are delinked from the real world and only make little use of historical data, they may fail to reflect dynamic characteristics of the real world [86]. In addition, apart from using the data for validation, the data may not influence the structure of the model [87].

3.2.2 Dynamic unidirectional data integration

The second approach entails a unidirectional flow of data from measuring systems to the simulation model. The data may capture the characteristics of the agents and be used to influence the dynamic behaviour of agents. For instance, taxi probe data may be gathered and be used to learn about agent characteristics and to implement a traffic-related simulation model [88]. However, the results from the simulation are not transferred to the measuring system to influence the data collection strategies. In addition, it is not necessary for the data to be recorded in real time. Data provides a means of extracting patterns that can then be used in ABM specification [72]. As an example, trajectories of animals, with precise spatial and temporal attributes can be used to infer patterns that may not be apparent in the domain knowledge [89]. The patterns from data can then be used to specify agent characteristics and to improve the model structure. An advantage of dynamic sensor data of this type lies in the repeated measurements of such data, which reveal the evolution of agent behaviour in space and time [90]. However, the simulation results are not compared to the real-time dynamics of the systems of interest; hence the model may still deviate from the reality.

3.2.3 Dynamic bidirectional data assimilation

In dynamic bidirectional data-driven models, real-time or near real-time sensor observations provide the empirical input that influence the simulation in real-time [21]. In the simplest form, data from the real world may only influence the characterisation of the modelling environment. For instance, real-time temperature and wind characteristics may be used to influence the environment of a model on fire dynamics [91, 92].

At the advanced level of dynamic data-driven simulation, output from the model can used to influence the sensor measurement strategies. For example, when modelling the influence of a hurricane, sensors in areas which are characterised by minimal intensity and impact of the hurricane both in the real world and in the model can be shut down or slowed down, while the frequency of data collection of sensors in high priority areas can be increased [93]. The bidirectional feedback improves both the data collection strategy and the accuracy of the models [94].

To facilitate the bidirectional communication between sensors and simulation models, dynamic data-driven systems adopt a three-step process consisting of sensing, prediction and adapting [95]. During sensing, sensors measure or record the entities of interest; simulation models then predict the probable change in the state of the entity. Finally, the sensing system is adapted to capture and validate the simulated state of the entities. This generic approach provides the foundational concepts for specification of dynamic data-driven agent-based model.

3.3 Dynamic data-driven agent-based models

Dynamic data-driven agent-based models remain one of the exemplary specifications of sensor data-driven ABMs. In this implementation, dynamic sensor data streams improve the specification of multi-agent systems, allowing models to benefit from the real-time behaviour and interactions between agents in a real-world setting. The main components of this framework include (i) the sensor measuring, which observe entities in the real world, providing a mirror of the happenings in the system of interest; (ii) data management system; (iii) modelling or simulation platform; and (iv) visualisation and dynamic communication suite. In some instances, the modelling platform may also serve as the visualisation interfaces.

Whereas the initial DDDABM implementations were ad hoc and relied on standards developed within the project or on widely recognised standards within computer science and engineering, the latter adaptations have utilised well-established standards by the Open Geospatial Consortium (OGC) to promote standardised discovery of sensor resources, documentation of sensor observations and uncertainties and transfer of outputs from modelling workflows [96]. Data management strategy can either be loosely coupled, distributed or centralised or adopt a complex negotiation between a distributed and centralised data management strategy.

3.4 Types of dynamic sensor data-driven applications for simulation

In an attempt to bridge the gap between models and real-world systems, different approaches have been proposed or adopted to incorporate dynamic sensor data into spatially explicit ABMs. The purpose of data integration influences the methods for the integration and the extent to which data is use used in the models. Some of the generic implementations include the following: (i) data-driven calibration of agent-based models, (ii) adaptive optimisation of model parameters, (iii) service-oriented architecture in geosimulation, (iv) agent parallelisation and dynamic visualisation, (v) dynamic data-driven multi-agent systems (DDDMAS) and (vi) adaptive discovery of models from sensor data streams.

While these categories may not be conclusive, they cover the main attributes of sensor data-driven spatial simulation models as will be specified in the following sections.

3.4.1 Data-driven calibration of spatial agent-based models

Conventionally, calibration of agent-based models aims to achieve two purposes. The first purpose is to find a robust and comprehensive list of parameters that can simulate the intended behaviours of a model. The second aim is to find optimal parameter ranges that can replicate the intended behaviours. Calibration is therefore an important step in model specification as it provides an idea of the essential parameters that affect agent behaviour while also providing the sensitivity ranges of these parameters. A properly calibrated model captures the essential dynamics of a system and can contribute towards achieving an accurate representation of the real world.

Traditionally, calibration of ABMs relies on historical data. However, in time-dependent and contextually sensitive systems like most of the spatial systems, historical data may not capture all the dynamics of a variant system. Consequently, calibration of models with historical data may cause the models to deviate from real-world realities. This is more so when the agents in the model face dynamics and situations that were absent in the historical data. Incorporating data from the real world during the model run can therefore provide a means of fine-tuning the model parameters to be reflective of the realities in the real-world scenarios [97]. For instance, when simulating road traffic, historical data may not have captured traffic jams that result from emergencies on the road, incorporating real-time data of such incidences when they occur can provide the necessary input to fine-tune the model parameters and to ensure the currency of model results.

To achieve dynamic calibration, it is important to have a systematic means of comparing model states against the real-world states. A proper scheduling scheme and tightly coupled link between the real-world schedule and the model schedule can help in deciding the calibration points. For instance, the schedule of sensor data collection and collation should be synchronised with the model time to allow for comparison between sensor observations and simulation results. It is therefore important to have an observation model from the sensor observation system that is comparable to the simulated results.

Dynamic calibration is achieved through methods of data assimilation which combine the state of the system as observed in the real world with the results from a simulation model in order to produce an improved prediction [98]. In particular, particle filter (PF) methods [99], for instance, Kalman filter (KF), have been used to assimilate data from pedestrian counts into a pedestrian simulation model [100]. In another example, Sequential Monte Carlo (SMC) method was used to assimilate sensor into building occupancy simulation [101].

For data assimilation, a proper sampling scheme allows for a randomised selection of data from the real world, and assimilating these with a sample of the simulation results to provide an updated state of model dynamics. Data assimilation improves the accuracy of the model as model parameters are updated to be in harmony with the patterns in the real world. However, models that are heavily reliant on data assimilation for the calibration of model parameters may run the risk of overfitting the model parameters to the data and therefore reduce the replicability of the models in data-deficient scenarios. Consequently, other methods which promote cross-validation [102] have been proposed as they go beyond dynamic calibration.

3.4.2 Adaptive optimisation and validation of model parameters

Discovery of representative parameters remains an outstanding challenge in the specification of data-driven spatial simulation models. This is more so when the velocity and volume of data collection outstrip the knowledge domain of the system of interest. When rich-annotated sensor data is available, multiple parameters may be inferred from the data. However, not all the parameters may be useful or adequately robust for representing the system of interest. Identifying robust and representative set of parameters for capturing the behaviour of the system of interest becomes a challenge. In addition, finding optimal parameter space for simulating the real-world system accurately can be challenging. Consequently, discovery and optimisation of parameters has been another aspect of dynamic data-driven simulation. Statistical methods including Markov chain [103] and its variants have been employed to discover initial parameters that may influence the dynamics of a model.

Evolutionary methods are suitable for dynamic optimisation of model parameters. In particular, genetic algorithms that borrow from biology have been employed to optimise parameters in data-driven ABMs [104, 105]. This has particularly been possible because of the adaptive nature of genetic algorithms which allows them to learn from data and to improve the specification of model parameters.

It is possible to implement dynamic calibration and optimisation of model parameters from a centralised data management system. However, the dynamic nature of sensor resources requires a service-oriented architecture to facilitate dynamic discovery, analysis and communication of sensor res using open and standardised protocols. Consequently, the development of various sensor resource management standards within OGC has promoted development of service-oriented architectures including Sensor Observation Service (SOS), Sensor Web Enablement (SWE) and other Geosensor Network Services that facilitate the discovery, access and computation on sensor resources in a standardised way. As a result, there have also been advances in sensor-oriented geosimulation frameworks.

3.4.3 Service-oriented geosimulation framework

In service-oriented geosimulation frameworks, sensor resources are specified as services that can be accessed and used in the model to achieve specific goals [106]. The adoption of sensor-oriented architecture in a dynamic data-driven ABM begins by considering Agents-as-a-Service (AaaS) [107]. In the approach, different aspects of the sensor data collection, management and computation system can be viewed in terms of their functionality [108]. The functionality defines the agency of these sensor network resources. For instance, sensor nodes whose role is to measure environmental characteristics exemplify measuring service hence can be specified as measuring agents.

Specification of sensor resources as services allows the elements of sensor network to be represented in the models as software agents. The behaviour and operations of sensor software agents can be simulated in parallel to other agents of interest in the system under analysis. For instance, in a hydrological network whose aim is to observe and analyse nutrient and sediment load in a catchment. Different sensors, for measuring environmental and hydrological characteristics, can be specified as agents in the model. Entities of interest, which may include water particles and sediment, can also be specified as autonomous agents. Specification of various sensor components as service agents in the model also allow for agent characteristics like autonomy, intelligence, interaction and adaptability to be included. Such agent characteristics can enhance the efficiency in the use of the sensor network resources and the versatility of the sensors in the model.

The service agents can provide the link between the real world and the simulation environment [109]. Specifically, the service agents capture information from the real world and execute the initial network level computations before relaying the processed information to fine-tune the specification of the model world while also providing information for dynamic calibration of the models. At the same time, specifying sensors as service agents in the model also makes it possible to influence the behaviour of such sensor agents, hence promoting a bidirectional communication between the model and the sensing system. This characteristic makes it possible to manipulate the sensor behaviour from the model.

In spite of the positive attributes of adopting a service-oriented geosimulation, challenges emerge in communication, computation, visualisation and data management, necessitating the refinement of the service-oriented approach and the development of other paradigms like agent parallelisation and dynamic visualisation.

3.4.4 Agent parallelisation and dynamic visualisation

Parallelisation improves efficiency in spatial explicit ABMs with thousands of agents and multiple interconnected tasks [110]. As an example, incorporation of sensor data into geosimulation models may require distributed data management, exploratory data analysis, pattern extraction, dynamic calibration, analysis of the model results and complex communication between different model components. The multiple tasks, particularly when the velocity of the data streams is high and the volume of the data is big, can limit the efficiency of the intended model. Consequently, parallelisation can improve the efficiency of modelling operations. Within sensor-driven agent-based systems, two common types of parallelisation in spatial ABM include agent parallelisation and environment parallelisation [111]. For models with multiple sub-models, a third type of parallelisation is known as task parallelisation.

3.4.4.1 Agent parallelisation

Agent parallelisation entails separating, distributing and simulating the behaviour of various agents in different cores. Individual cores keep track of agent properties and spatial locations. In ecology, agent parallelisation has been implemented to simulate predator–prey models [112].

3.4.4.2 Environment parallelisation

Environment parallelisation involves breaking an expansive modelling world into multiple smaller spatial units or tiles and distributing the small units to different cores. Simulation can then proceed in each core. One challenge in this kind of setup is in simulating mobile agents that move extensively across the area of study.

3.4.4.3 Task parallelisation

Task parallelisation involves breaking down modelling tasks into different modular operations that can be performed in parallel in different cores [113]. For instance, an agent-based model can be broken down into sub-models that can run concurrently on parallelised cores. This kind of setup can also help in solving scheduling questions and can improve efficiency of simulation.

Important components of an effective parallelisation include distributed data management system, high-performance geosimulation environment which includes modules for specification of agency and a dynamic geo-visualisation platform [114]. The performance of the parallelisation scheme can be leveraged on open standards that facilitate distributed database management system, efficient communication [115], high-performance geosimulation and cyberGIS [116].

3.4.5 Dynamic data-driven multi-agent systems (DDDMAS)

Dynamic data-driven multi-agent systems are a modification of dynamic data-driven applications systems [21]. The initial motivation of DDDAS was to support the implementation of dynamic environmental monitoring systems incorporating different application systems with real-time data from the system of interest. An important attribute of the DDDAS is the possibility of bidirectional communication between sensors and models, which allows sensors to provide data from the real world for assimilation into models, hence improving the reliability of the models. On the other hand, simulation results influence the sensor measurement strategies.

In DDDMAS, the concepts from DDDAS are adopted in a multi-agent system to improve the specification and accuracy of multi-agent models [117]. In particular, sensors capture individual agent characteristics, hence facilitating the specification of agents. In addition, other sensors can capture environmental characteristics, hence ensuring that the environment in which the agents interact is dynamic and representative of the reality. On the other hand, the model outcomes influence sensor measurement strategies by promoting priority sensor deployment depending on the scenarios in the model. In spatial models, sensor network components and other entities in the model can be represented as autonomous, which can be identified by their unique geographic characteristics [118].

Apart from placing the sensors on the environment, on-body sensors [119] can provide both the contextual and physiological characteristics of agents that may be important in understanding ambient behaviours of the simulated agents. To get the best out of the sensor agents, sensors should not only be measuring devices but must also be cognitive [120]. Cognitive sensor agents can have a mental state which may include intelligence, computational ability and decision-making components [20]. Other attributes that such cognitive agents may have include self-organisation, learning and adaptability. These attributes allow the sensors to gather information (both from the environment and from the models), analyse such information and make autonomous decisions that improve the data collection strategies and facilitate the specification of accurate models.

3.4.6 Dynamic discovery of models from sensor data

The most advanced level of dynamic data-driven simulation entails the discovery of rulesets and algorithms that make up accurate simulation models. The process of model specification can be arduous especially when there is vague knowledge about the system of interest. Automated discovery of robust algorithms, which are capable of representing the dynamics of a system of interest, is therefore a giant leap in the epistemology of agent-based simulations [121].

The essential building blocks of agent-based models are the entities, interactions and contextual information that influence entity decisions and interactions. Data containing detailed characteristics of the entities, their interactions and the contextual information in the environment where they operate may provide an avenue for discovering behavioural models of the agents, hence facilitating automated model specification.

Capturing the cognitive characteristics of humans and animals remains a challenge both technically and due to ethical reasons. However, recent advances in biosensor technology have made it possible to capture nonintrusive physiological characteristics which can then be related to the emotional and mental state of humans [122] and animals. Data on such cognitive characteristics of agents can facilitate in understanding and specifying the motivation of agents. In robotics and unmanned aerial vehicles (UAV), sensors can also be used to capture information for building the intelligence of the robotics and of the UAVs [123]. Such agents therefore need an additional capability of learning, hence building their knowledge beyond the hard-wired artificial intelligence. The learned knowledge can improve swarm intelligence in UAVs, safety in self-driving cars and efficiency in adaptive industrial processes.

Because of the dynamic nature of data and complexities of the spatial environments, understanding of the agent decisions and the emergence of system-level characteristics requires an automated model discovery. One suggestion for generating spatial rulesets for multi-agent systems is the global-to-local programming approach [124]. The approach attempts to decompose a programming task into individual simple spatial dimensions and then generate candidate rulesets for each dimension. The dimensions may include configuration, local rules, timing, patterns and robustness. Genetic algorithm can then be used to combine and evolve the candidate sub-models resulting in a robust rulesets that can simulate the multi-agent system of interest [121].

Other implementations involve implementing methods from machine learning to discover an initial population of algorithms from a solution space [125]. The initial population of algorithms can then be optimised using genetic algorithms to produce the most efficient combination of algorithms that can simulate the system of interest. The result is an adaptive ruleset, which is not handicapped by the domain knowledge but that emerges based on the richness of solution space. The richness of the solution space depends on the diversity of data from various sensor data streams. Automated discovery of models can reduce the time spent in model specification and result in behaviours that can be described mathematically, hence improving the conceptualisation of agent behaviours. Consequently, such modelling workflows can contribute to automated knowledge discovery.

As has been outlined in this section, tremendous progress has been made to facilitate dynamic data integration into agent-based models. The progress is bound to shorten modelling cycle and to improve accuracy of ABMs by ensuring the fidelity of the models to the dynamic sensor observations in the real world. However, dependence on data may come with the challenge of model overfitting. Similarly, unless proper flexibility is allowed in the parameter estimation and model discovery, data-driven models can end up as "black box" models, which, even though may lead to accurate results, do not allow users to understand how the optimised parameters and adaptive algorithms emerge. In order to contribute to addressing the challenge of model overfitting, we see potential solutions in leveraging the specification of sensor-driven spatially explicit models on well-established guidelines like pattern-oriented modelling, service-oriented architecture, parallelisation and optimisation of various model components through evolutionary algorithms. In the following section, a conceptual framework for sensor-driven spatially explicit model is provided.

4. Framework for dynamic sensor-driven spatially explicit agent-based models

An accurate, spatially explicit, agent-based model should aim at replicating all the essential patterns of the system by simulating the local behaviour of agents. Pattern or behaviour detection is therefore an important component of data-driven simulation models [126]. Consequently, in order to specify accurate models, the modelling workflow requires a module to facilitate pattern extraction in order to discover multi-scale patterns from the sensor data streams. The patterns can drive dynamic calibration and validation of the model. Because of the velocity and dynamic nature of sensor observations, bridging the gap between sensor observations and model specification necessitates the processes of calibration and validation to be closer and tied tightly to the simulation processes. This is in contrast to the conventional methods where specification, calibration and validation are sequential steps that are implemented at separate times. The challenge thus is to decide on a suitable pattern-oriented modelling strategy in which the patterns from sensor data streams are separated into specification, calibration and validation patterns. **Figure 3** provides the conceptual framework for sensor-driven spatial simulation model.

In the conceptual model, there are three important layers in the dynamic simulation life cycle. The three are the observation layer, exploratory analysis layer and the simulation layer.

4.1 Observation layer

The observation layer specifies the data collection and management strategy. In particular, the layer specifies the sensor-driven observation experiment and the associated sensor and network infrastructure that facilitate accurate, complete and efficient data collection and preprocessing. The preprocessing step may include spatial and temporal sampling of the sensor observations to capture only the important attributes of the agents of interest. In order to address the spatial questions that are the focus of spatial simulation modelling, observations should include both the spatial characteristics such as the location and time and other agents and environment-specific data. Consequently, standards from OGC Geosensor Network Services can

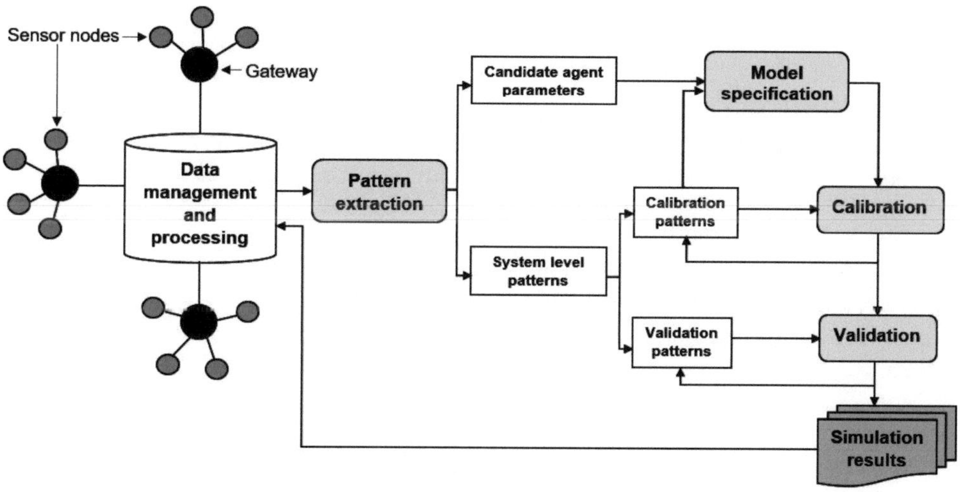

Figure 3.
Proposed conceptual model for dynamic data-driven spatially explicit ABM. Geosensors capture data on the dynamics of the agents including their behaviour characteristics, space use and interactions. Preliminary on-site computation can be executed within the sensor networks before the data is parsed onto a data management and processing unit. Apart from storing the data in an efficient manner, the processing unit provides applications that can facilitate communication between the simulation model and the sensor network. The second process in the workflow involves exploratory data analysis and pattern extraction which results in an exhaustive list of system-level patterns and potential parameters that can be used to create a population of solutions for specifying the ABM. In addition, exploratory analysis reveals the tentative temporal steps at which it may be possible to identify micro level patterns of the system of interest. The patterns are separated into calibration and validation categories. The calibration patterns are hard-wired into the model through evolutionary optimisation of the candidate parameters. A specified model is calibrated dynamically and iteratively during the model. Once an adequate number of calibration steps have been executed, dynamic validation is initiated and is based on the reserve patterns that were not initially hard-wired into the model. The simulation outcome resulting from the validation stage is transferred to the data processing unit for assimilation with "fresh" data from the sensor observations. The process is cyclic and continues until the model accurately reproduces all the patterns in the data.

be adopted to guide the sensor selection and data collection processes. In addition, open standards that promote interoperability and transfer of sensor data and other resources should be encouraged. In particular, the use of Observation and Measurement (O&M) specification can facilitate both the documentation of data and uncertainties associated with the data. This is important for communicating the provenance of uncertainty throughout the modelling cycle.

For the data management, a distributed spatio-temporal database [114] is preferable when the study area is expansive and when there may be a need to carry out on-site quality assessment of the data from various sensor networks. Otherwise, a centralised Sensor Web Enablement (SWE) platform allowing for seamless discovery and manipulation and transfer of data and resources through standardised OGC compliant specifications is the most reliable. Examples of agent-oriented middleware for decentralised dynamic data collection include Sensomax [127], SenseWare [128] and MAPS [129]. Standardised data management systems facilitate characterisation of agent behaviours, multi-tasking and bidirectional communication between different components of the simulation workflow and the sensor nodes.

Apart from the geosensor data, additional spatial data from standard GIS data models and remote sensing products can be incorporated into the data management system to boost the characterisation of the environment in which the agents operate. For instance, when simulating dynamics of environmental changes, spatial data including human population and settlement, land use characteristics, topography, accessibility, vegetation indices, land surface temperature (LST), fire occurrence, night-time light, aerosols etc. can be combined with the in situ sensor data to provide a rich characterisation of the modelling world.

4.2 Exploratory analysis layer

The strength of data-driven models lies in the robust discovery of distinctive spatial and temporal patterns in the sensor data streams. Such patterns may be indicative of the essential processes and dynamics of the system of interest. The exploratory analysis is therefore a critical stage where statistical and machine-learning methods are applied to extract multi-scale patterns and other important characteristic parameters which may facilitate an accurate specification and simulation of the system behaviours. In situations where some knowledge has been documented concerning the system under study, then such information can guide and improve the pattern extraction process.

Statistical methods including multi-scale clustering and classification have been employed to reveal clusters in the data. For instance, in animal movement, Expectation–Maximization Binary Clustering (EMBC) [130] method has been applied to detect specific spatial and temporal navigation behaviours of birds. In human mobility trajectory analysis, DBSCAN clustering method has been applied to find traffic patterns [131]. Similarly, in flocking and swarm behaviour models, Spatial Clustering Algorithm Through Swarm Intelligence (SPARROW) clustering method has been used [132]. In addition, spatio-temporal data analysis methods including Bayesian spatio-temporal partitioning and clustering methods can be implemented to reveal the variation in behaviour of agents and the dynamics of the system in both space and time. Apart from statistical methods, machine-learning methods including convolutional neural networks (CNN), artificial neural network (ANN) and deep learning have been applied to reveal patterns. The use of mathematical and computational methods has the advantage that resulting patterns can be explicitly defined, hence building a mathematical or computational conceptualisation of such patterns [125]. The patterns can also provide a hint of agent processes that are inherent in the systems of interest.

In addition to the patterns, exploratory analysis process identifies essential parameters behind the patterns and processes of the system, allowing for specification of model parameters and identification of potential behaviour characteristics. Parameters are independent variables that influence the local-level behaviour of the agents. Related to the parameters, the exploratory analysis should also identify appropriate simulation schedules to facilitate the replication of all the necessary multi-scale patterns. An appropriate scheduling scheme also ensures the efficiency of the computation by informing a realistic temporal scale for the model and limiting unnecessary iteration of model runs.

Further, the exploratory analysis should also identify potential variables to be specified as the state variables of the agents. State variables are the agent-specific characteristics that vary dynamically in the model. State variables are essential as they provide a way of comparing the simulated agents against real-world agents while also providing a means of understanding how the local agent variables contribute to the multi-scale patterns. As an output from the exploratory process, a modeller should have an extensive list of potential model parameters and patterns that are essential for understanding the dynamics of the system. It is at this point that patterns should clearly be separated into the calibration and the validation patterns in preparation for their use in the dynamic simulation process.

4.3 Simulation layer

The simulation layer entails dynamic model specification, calibration and validation steps. As opposed to the conventional static ABMs, the specification, calibration and validation steps of a dynamic sensor-driven model can be implemented dynamically and iteratively during a single runtime and may run concurrently in a parallelised system.

In the model specification stage, the first step is to decide on a mechanism of combining or reducing the population of parameters into a robust set that can drive the essential behaviour of the agents. Evolutionary computation methods have been effective particularly in optimising ABM parameters [133]. One common example of evolutionary method for data-driven simulation is genetic algorithms [134]. In genetic algorithm, a random combination of the parameters can be created for each agent to provide the initial solution space [135]. The solution space evolves chromosomal crossover and mutation, which are critical operators of a genetic algorithm.

Further, to generate robust parameters, a proper fitness function should be derived to provide a basis of comparing the performance of the simulated agents against their real-world counterparts. A simple approach involves deriving fitness function a function of the variance between state variables and empirical agent characteristics. However, such a fitness function may increase the risk of model overfitting as the simulated agents are forced to replicate specific stepwise processes that are captured in the data. Consequently, deriving a fitness as a function from patterns may relax the focus from the state variables to the flexible multi-scale patterns. In addition, the combination of multiple patterns in defining fitness function can lead to generic and robust fitness functions. This is because patterns are generic spatial and temporal footprint that can be observed and described in the data.

Adopting a pattern-oriented modelling approach ensures that the process of model specification, calibration and validation is driven by the patterns that are inherent in the dynamic data. Consequently, this reduces the risk of tying the model parameters to the data, hence limiting the chance of model overfitting. In addition, since validation patterns are not explicitly hard-coded into the model, rigorously validated data-driven models can help in explaining the agent dynamics that lead to multi-scale patterns. The results of a properly calibrated and dynamically validated model can be parsed to the central data management and processing unit for data assimilation and to influence the behaviour of the observation and measurement layer in cases where this is necessary. The cyclic communication between sensor observations and assimilation of simulation results bridges the gap between sensor data measurements and model specification and facilitates a mutually beneficial feedback between sensing unit and simulation model.

5. Outlook and potential applications of sensor data-driven spatially explicit ABMs

Advances in sensor technology, particularly the miniaturisation and ubiquity of sensors have led to an exponential growth in the diversity of the fine-scaled data, which can facilitate model specifications. In geographic information science, in situ sensor data provide accurate measurements of spatial entities and augment other data from earth observation workflows in characterising the environment in which agents interact. Sensor data therefore plays an important role in capturing the dynamics that cause spatial and temporal patterns. Accurate sensor data contributes towards understanding local-level interactions of humans, animals, firms, smart appliances and traffic, and the role of such interactions in global environmental changes. Similarly, the application of sensors has been a major driver in pervasive geographic information systems [136, 137] including in indoor environments and in the internet of things (IoT), technologies that are relevant for smart building and facility management.

However, advances in tools and software to support dynamic spatially explicit ABM specification have not been in tandem to the progress in sensor observation systems. Common ABM software including NetLogo, SWARM, MASON and Repast can handle only desktop-based geospatial data models. GAMA [138], which has the most extensive suite of tools for geospatial data handling and manipulation, does not have an equally extensive suite of APIs that can support dynamic data injection from sensor data streams, while FRAME and Repast HPC, which even though can support specification and simulation of distributed ABM, are not open and widely accessible. Moreover, most implementations of dynamic sensor-driven ABMs have been implemented to meet the objectives of specific projects and mainly in the computer science community and in the sensor (or geosensor) community. It is therefore important that modellers and practitioners in spatial simulation should develop reliable tools that can allow ABMs to be fed with rich sensor data streams from the systems of interest.

Potential areas of application of dynamic sensor-driven spatially explicit include animal ecology, human mobility studies and particularly in understanding mobility patterns and use of urban environment, energy use, indoor positioning systems, fire behaviour modelling, tourism research military applications, smart agriculture, environmental monitoring and in automation of industrial processes.

Epistemologically, the emergence of methods for data-driven ABMs raises questions on the place of conventional ABMs. In particular, do the data-driven models radically change the epistemological underpinnings of traditional ABM modelling framework? In other words, can accurate models be specified without relying on the domain knowledge and expertise of the modellers? To this question, a cautious approach should be encouraged. Whereas data-driven models are promising particularly in specifying models for theory-poor systems, a hybrid approach that starts from the domain knowledge and augments such knowledge with well-structured data-driven methods can improve reliability of agent-based simulation. Domain knowledge can provide the foundational understanding of a system of interest, while rich and dynamic data can provide a means of discovering detailed local-level patterns and parameters of the system. In addition, results from data-driven models can augment domain knowledge. In a nutshell, data should help in defining the crisp concepts and in discovering hidden characteristics of the systems when these are not apparent in the domain knowledge. Consequently, as the data continues to grow in scale, accuracy and volume, while methods for big data analysis become more robust, data-driven models can be expected to grow and augment knowledge discovery in theory-poor domains. Sensor-driven spatially explicit ABMs therefore have an important role to play in understanding and representing dynamic spatial processes.

6. Conclusion

The aim of this paper was to trace and document the progress in the methods for specifying data-driven ABMs for spatial systems. In particular, the focus here has been on models that are fed with data from dynamic sensor data streams. It is clear from the documentation that advances in sensor and wireless communication technology have contributed immensely to the growth of data-driven ABMs. Data has been used in initialising, calibrating and validating models. However, traditionally, historical data has been fed into the models only sparingly without considering the dynamic changes in the real world. Though the conventional ABMs have been effective in generating hypothesis and representing dynamics of knowledge-rich systems, they have not been very applicable in addressing questions in complex and adaptive spatial systems whose internal dynamics are yet to be well understood. Moreover, the weakness of ABMs in predicting future states of systems persists. Designing accurate models for such systems can therefore be leveraged on the rich sensor data streams.

In this work, we proposed a framework for pattern-oriented, sensor-driven and spatially explicit ABM. In the framework, the steps of model specification, calibration and validation are implemented dynamically during the model run and are facilitated by patterns that can be derived dynamically from sensor data. This approach could contribute towards addressing the challenges of model overfitting that face most data-driven models. By validating models based on validation patterns that are not explicitly hard-coded into the model, the framework ensures that model parameters are not tied merely to the data but that the parameters and behaviours of the model can replicate patterns that are evident in the data. Most importantly, to promote efficient communication and management of sensor resources, we propose a service-oriented framework where sensor and network components are represented in the model as software agents in parallel to agents representing other real-world entities. This kind of arrangement allows well-known standards like the OGC standards of sensor specification to be applied in the modelling process, hence promoting discoverability and interoperability of sensor and model resources.

The main limitation of this review was in the fact that we did not include a prototype to demonstrate the practical application of the framework. However, examples can be seen in 4D-SAS [114] and DDDMAS application. Future research should include developing open and efficient tools that can promote distributed processing, simulation and visualisation of sensor-driven ABMs. Moreover, as behaviour specification has been one of the daunting tasks in typical ABM specification, automate discovery of algorithms from dynamic sensor data streams remains an exciting area of research that requires additional research. Robust methods for automated model discovery will improve the efficiency of data-driven spatial simulation models.

Epistemologically, sensor data-driven models raise important questions on the role of data in the specification of spatial simulation models. As geographic information science is an emerging field. It is our view that data-driven spatial simulation models will not only rely on the domain knowledge but will also contribute to methods of knowledge discovery in the field. As such, specification of ABMs can no longer merely rely on the domain knowledge but must be leveraged on the big data resources that are emerging from various advances in technology and computation. However, caution should be taken to allow a systematic development of data-driven methods in spatial simulation. Presently, we recommend a hybrid approaches that combine both domain knowledge and data-driven methods. Such models could be improved by relying on patterns that are extracted dynamically from sensor data streams.

Acknowledgements

This research was funded by the Austrian Science Fund (FWF) through the Doctoral College GIScience at the University of Salzburg (DK W 1237-N23).

Author details

Francis Oloo[1,2]

1 Doctoral College of GIScience (DK GIScience), University of Salzburg, Salzburg, Austria

2 The Technical University of Kenya, Nairobi, Kenya

*Address all correspondence to: oloofrank@gmail.com

References

[1] Bonabeau E. Agent-based modeling: Methods and techniques for simulating human systems. Proceedings of the National Academy of Sciences. 2002;**99**(Suppl 3):7280-7287

[2] Janssen MA, Ostrom E. Empirically based, agent-based models. Ecology and Society 2006;**11**(2):37. Available from: http://www.ecologyandsociety.org/vol11/iss2/art37/

[3] McLane AJ et al. The role of agent-based models in wildlife ecology and management. Ecological Modelling. 2011;**222**(8):1544-1556

[4] An L. Modeling human decisions in coupled human and natural systems: Review of agent-based models. Ecological Modelling. 2012;**229**:25-36

[5] Ajelli M et al. Spatiotemporal dynamics of the Ebola epidemic in Guinea and implications for vaccination and disease elimination: A computational modeling analysis. BMC Medicine. 2016;**14**(1):130

[6] Alderton S et al. A multi-host agent-based model for a zoonotic, vector-borne disease. A case study on Trypanosomiasis in Eastern Province, Zambia. PLoS Neglected Tropical Diseases. 2016;**10**(12):e0005252

[7] Venkatramanan S et al. Using data-driven agent-based models for forecasting emerging infectious diseases. Epidemics. 2018;**22**:43-49

[8] Fang Z et al. Agent-based simulation analysis on the effect of an LNG terminal on a port transport system. In: CICTP 2014: Safe, Smart, and Sustainable Multimodal Transportation Systems—Proceedings of the 14th COTA International Conference of Transportation Professionals. 2014

[9] Fernández-Isabel A, Fuentes-Fernández R. Analysis of intelligent transportation systems using model-driven simulations. Sensors (Switzerland). 2015;**15**(6):14117-14141

[10] Jensen T, Chappin ÉJL. Automating agent-based modeling: Data-driven generation and application of innovation diffusion models. Environmental Modelling and Software. 2017;**92**:261-268

[11] Castella JC, Verburg PH. Combination of process-oriented and pattern-oriented models of land-use change in a mountain area of Vietnam. Ecological Modelling. 2007;**202**(3-4):410-420

[12] Hanappi G. Agent-based modelling. History, essence, future. PSL Quarterly Review. 2017;**70**(283):449-472

[13] Bruch E, Atwell J. Agent-based models in empirical social research. Sociological Methods & Research. 2015;**44**(2):186-221

[14] MacBride RAF. Applying Systems Science Methods to Risk-Based Disease Management and Population Oral Health. Los Angeles: University of California; 2018

[15] Drchal J, Čertický M, Jakob M. Data driven validation framework for multi-agent activity-based models. In: International Workshop on Multi-Agent Systems and Agent-Based Simulation. Springer; 2015

[16] Arifin S, Davis GJ, Zhou Y. Modeling space in an agent-based model of malaria: Comparison between non-spatial and spatial models. In: Proceedings of the 2011 Workshop on Agent-Directed Simulation. Society for Computer Simulation International; 2011

[17] Nittel S. A survey of geosensor networks: Advances in dynamic environmental monitoring. Sensors. 2009;**9**(7):5664-5678

[18] Bergmann JH et al. Exploring the use of sensors to measure behavioral interactions: An experimental evaluation of using hand trajectories. PLoS One. 2014;**9**(2):e88080

[19] Harari GM et al. Using smartphones to collect behavioral data in psychological science: Opportunities, practical considerations, and challenges. Perspectives on Psychological Science. 2016;**11**(6):838-854

[20] Niazi MA, Hussain A. A novel agent-based simulation framework for sensing in complex adaptive environments. IEEE Sensors Journal. 2011;**11**(2):404-412

[21] Darema F. Dynamic data driven applications systems: New capabilities for application simulations and measurements. In: International Conference on Computational Science. Springer; 2005

[22] Ha SW et al. An environmental monitoring system for managing spatiotemporal sensor data over sensor networks. Sensors. 2012;**12**(4):3997-4015

[23] Bröring A et al. New generation sensor web enablement. Sensors. 2011;**11**(3):2652-2699

[24] Saha D, Mukherjee A. Pervasive computing: A paradigm for the 21st century. Computer. 2003;**36**(3):25-31

[25] Want HWGR, Schmidt A. Pervasive computing. IEEE. 2006;**5**:25-33

[26] Anselin L. What is special about spatial data? Alternative Perspectives on Spatial Data Analysis (89-4). 1989

[27] Liu Y et al. Towards a rich-context participatory cyber environment. International Workshop on Grid Computing environment. Reno, NV, USA; 2007

[28] Hart G, Dolbear C. What's so special about spatial? In: The Geospatial Web. Springer; 2009. pp. 39-44

[29] Gotelli NJ et al. Patterns and causes of species richness: A general simulation model for macroecology. Ecology Letters. 2009;**12**(9):873-886

[30] O'Sullivan D, Perry GL. Spatial Simulation: Exploring Pattern and Process. West Sussex, UK: John Wiley & Sons; 2013

[31] Rodrigues A, Raper J. Defining spatial agents. In: Taylor, Francis Editors. London, United Kingdom: Spatial Multimedia and Virtual Reality; 1999:111-129

[32] Itami RM. Mobile Agents with Spatial Intelligence. Oxford, UK: Oxford University Press; 2002

[33] Sajjad M et al. A data-driven approach for agent-based modeling: Simulating the dynamics of family formation. Journal of Artificial Societies and Social Simulation. 2016;**19**(1):9

[34] Brown DG et al. Path dependence and the validation of agent-based spatial models of land use. International Journal of Geographical Information Science. 2005;**19**(2):153-174

[35] Poza DJ et al. Mesoscopic effects in an agent-based bargaining model in regular lattices. PLoS One. 2011;**6**(3):e17661

[36] Fonoberova M et al. An agent-based model of urban insurgence: Effect of gathering sites and Koopman mode analysis. PLoS One. 2018;**13**(10):e0205259

[37] Filatova T et al. Spatial agent-based models for socio-ecological systems: Challenges and prospects.

Environmental Modelling & Software. 2013;**45**:1-7

[38] Brown DG et al. Spatial process and data models: Toward integration of agent-based models and GIS. Journal of Geographical Systems. 2005;7(1):25-47

[39] Nagy M et al. Hierarchical group dynamics in pigeon flocks. Nature. 2010;**464**(7290):890

[40] Vhaduri S et al. Estimating drivers' stress from GPS traces. In: Proceedings of the 6th International Conference on Automotive User Interfaces and Interactive Vehicular Applications. ACM; 2014

[41] Al-Husain L, Kanjo E, Chamberlain A. Sense of space: Mapping physiological emotion response in urban space. In: Proceedings of the 2013 ACM Conference on Pervasive and Ubiquitous Computing Adjunct Publication. ACM; 2013

[42] Pharow P et al. Portable devices. In: Sensors and Networks: Wireless Personalized eHealth Services. Amsterdam, Netherlands: IOS Press; 2009

[43] Grimm V, Railsback SF. Individual-based Modeling and Ecology. Princeton NJ, USA: Princeton University Press; 2013

[44] Barnes DJ, Chu D. Guide to Simulation and Modeling for Biosciences. London, UK: Springer; 2015

[45] Marschak J. Economic measurements for policy and prediction. In: Economic Information, Decision, and Prediction. Dordrecht, Netherlands: Springer; 1974. pp. 293-322

[46] Grimm V et al. Pattern-oriented modeling of agent-based complex systems: Lessons from ecology. Science. 2005;**310**(5750):987-991

[47] Ormerod P, Rosewell B. Validation and Verification of Agent-Based Models in the Social Sciences. Berlin, Heidelberg: Springer Berlin Heidelberg; 2009

[48] Niazi MA, Hussain A, Kolberg M. Verification & validation of agent based simulations using the VOMAS (virtual overlay multi-agent system) approach. arXiv preprint arXiv:1708.02361. 2017

[49] Windrum P, Fagiolo G, Moneta A. Empirical validation of agent-based models: Alternatives and prospects. Journal of Artificial Societies and Social Simulation. 2007;**10**(2):8

[50] Augusiak J, Van den Brink PJ, Grimm V. Merging validation and evaluation of ecological models to 'evaludation': A review of terminology and a practical approach. Ecological Modelling. 2014;**280**:117-128

[51] Grimm V et al. Towards better modelling and decision support: Documenting model development, testing, and analysis using TRACE. Ecological Modelling. 2014;**280**:129-139

[52] Müller B et al. Standardised and transparent model descriptions for agent-based models: Current status and prospects. Environmental Modelling & Software. 2014;**55**:156-163

[53] Grimm V, Schmolke A. How to read and write TRACE documentations. Leipzig, Germany: Helmholtz Centre for Environmental Research-UFZ. 2011 Available from: http://cream-itn.eu/creamwp/wp-content/uploads/Trace-Guidance-11-03-04.pdf

[54] Grimm V et al. The ODD protocol: A review and first update. Ecological Modelling. 2010;**221**(23):2760-2768

[55] Grimm V et al. A standard protocol for describing individual-based and agent-based models. Ecological Modelling. 2006;**198**(1-2):115-126

[56] Arroyo J et al. Re-thinking simulation: A methodological approach for the application of data mining in agent-based modelling. Computational and Mathematical Organization Theory. 2010;**16**(4):416-435

[57] Conte R, Paolucci M. On agent-based modeling and computational social science. Frontiers in Psychology. 2014;**5**:668

[58] Flack A et al. Costs of migratory decisions: A comparison across eight white stork populations. Science Advances. 2016;**2**(1):e1500931

[59] Ilie S, Bădică C. Multi-agent approach to distributed ant colony optimization. Science of Computer Programming. 2013;**78**(6):762-774

[60] Ilie S, Bădică C. Multi-agent distributed framework for swarm intelligence. Procedia Computer Science. 2013;**18**:611-620

[61] Beekman M, Sword GA, Simpson SJ. Biological foundations of swarm intelligence. In: Swarm Intelligence. Berlin, Heidelberg, Germany: Springer; 2008. pp. 3-41

[62] Bonabeau E, Corne D, Poli R. Swarm intelligence: The state of the art special issue of natural computing. Natural Computing. 2010;**9**(3):655-657

[63] Mishra BSP, Dehuri S, Wang G-N. A state-of-the-art review of artificial bee colony in the optimization of single and multiple criteria. International Journal of Applied Metaheuristic Computing (IJAMC). 2013;**4**(4):23-45

[64] Ahmad R et al. A multi-agent based approach for particle swarm optimization. In: 2007 International Conference on Integration of Knowledge Intensive Multi-Agent Systems. IEEE; 2007

[65] Bertsimas D, Jaillet P, Martin S. Online vehicle routing: The edge of optimization in large-scale applications. Operations Research. 2019;**67**(1):143-162

[66] Bai Q. Analysis of particle swarm optimization algorithm. Computer and Information Science. 2010;**3**(1):180

[67] Bürkle A, Segor F, Kollmann M. Towards autonomous micro uav swarms. Journal of Intelligent & Robotic Systems. 2011;**61**(1-4):339-353

[68] Hassan S et al. Stepping on earth: A roadmap for data-driven agent-based Modelling. In: Proceedings of the 5th Conference of the European Social Simulation Association (ESSA08). 2008

[69] Epstein JM. Agent-based computational models and generative social science. Complexity. 1999;**4**(5):41-60

[70] Heath B, Hill R, Ciarallo F. A survey of agent-based modeling practices (January 1998 to July 2008). Journal of Artificial Societies and Social Simulation. 2009;**12**(4):9

[71] Kavak H et al. Big data, agents, and machine learning: Towards a data-driven agent-based modeling approach. In: Proceedings of the Annual Simulation Symposium. Society for Computer Simulation International; 2018

[72] Zhong J et al. Learning behavior patterns from video for agent-based crowd modeling and simulation. Autonomous Agents and Multi-Agent Systems. 2016;**30**(5):990-1019

[73] Zhang H et al. Data-driven agent-based modeling, with application

to rooftop solar adoption. In: Proceedings of the 2015 International Conference on Autonomous Agents and Multiagent Systems. Istanbul, Turkey: International Foundation for Autonomous Agents and Multiagent Systems; 2015. pp. 513-521

[74] Pruyt E et al. From data-poor to data-rich: System dynamics in the era of big data. In: 32nd International Conference of the System Dynamics Society, Delft, The Netherlands, 20-24 July 2014; Authors Version. The System Dynamics Society; 2014

[75] Michopoulos J et al. Agent-based simulation of data-driven fire propagation dynamics. In: International Conference on Computational Science. Springer; 2004

[76] Goodchild MF. Geographic information systems and science: Today and tomorrow. Annals of GIS. 2009;**15**(1):3-9

[77] Nadi S, Delavar MR. Spatio-temporal modeling of dynamic phenomena in GIS. In: ScanGIS, Espoo, Finland; 2003. pp. 215-225

[78] Wang F, Zhou C, Nie Y. Event processing in sensor streams. In: Managing and Mining Sensor Data. Boston MA, USA: Springer; 2013. pp. 77-102

[79] Song J et al. Application of dynamic data driven application system in environmental science. Environmental Reviews. 2014;**22**(3):287-297

[80] Nittel S et al. Shared ride trip planning with geosensor networks. In: Societies and Cities in the Age of Instant Access. Dordrecht, Netherlands: Springer; 2007. pp. 179-194

[81] Sagl G, Resch B, Blaschke T. Contextual sensing: Integrating contextual information with human and technical geo-sensor information for smart cities. Sensors. 2015;**15**(7):17013-17035

[82] Hernández-Pliego J et al. Combined use of tri-axial accelerometers and GPS reveals the flexible foraging strategy of a bird in relation to weather conditions. PLoS One. 2017;**12**(6):e0177892

[83] Júnior JF et al. Driver behavior profiling: An investigation with different smartphone sensors and machine learning. PLoS One. 2017;**12**(4):e0174959

[84] Sahli N, Jabeur N, Badra M. Agent-based framework for sensor-to-sensor personalization. Procedia Computer Science. 2013;**19**:197-205

[85] Dagdeviren O et al. A survey of agent technologies for wireless sensor networks. IETE Technical Review. 2011;**28**(2):168-184

[86] Wang Z. Integrating spatio-temporal data into agent-based simulation for emergency navigation support. GISt Rapport, No. 58. 2012

[87] Kennedy C et al. AIMSS: An architecture for data driven simulations in the social sciences. In: International Conference on Computational Science. Berlin Heidelberg, Germany: Springer; 2007

[88] Ranjit S et al. Agent-based modeling of taxi behavior simulation with probe vehicle data. ISPRS International Journal of Geo-Information. 2018;**7**(5):177

[89] Bonnell TR et al. Emergent group level navigation: An agent-based evaluation of movement patterns in a folivorous primate. PLoS One. 2013;**8**(10):e78264

[90] Scheutz M, Mayer T. Combining agent-based modeling with big data methods to support architectural and urban design. In: Understanding

Complex Urban Systems. Cham, Switzerland: Springer; 2016. pp. 15-31

[91] Hu X. Dynamic data driven simulation. SCS M&S Magazine. 2011;**5**:16-22

[92] Rodríguez R, Cortés A, Margalef T. Injecting dynamic real-time data into a DDDAS for forest fire behavior prediction. In: International Conference on Computational Science. Springer; 2009

[93] Allen G. Building a dynamic data driven application system for hurricane forecasting. In: International Conference on Computational Science. Springer; 2007

[94] Darema F. Dynamic Data Driven Applications Systems: A New Paradigm for Application Simulations and Measurements. Berlin, Heidelberg: Springer Berlin Heidelberg; 2004

[95] Fujimoto R et al. A Dynamic Data Driven Application System for Vehicle Tracking. Procedia Computer Science; 2014;**29**(1):1203-1215

[96] Castrillón M et al. Forecasting and visualization of wildfires in a 3D geographical information system. Computers & Geosciences. 2011;**37**(3):390-396

[97] Heppenstall A, Malleson N, Crooks A. "Space, the final frontier": How good are agent-based models at simulating individuals and space in cities? Systems. 2016;**4**(1):9

[98] Rai S, Hu X. Behavior pattern detection for data assimilation in agent-based simulation of smart environments. In: Web Intelligence (WI) and Intelligent Agent Technologies (IAT), 2013 IEEE/WIC/ACM International Joint Conferences on. IEEE; 2013

[99] Xue H, Gu F, Hu X. Data assimilation using sequential Monte Carlo methods in wildfire spread simulation. ACM Transactions on Modeling and Computer Simulation (TOMACS). 2012;**22**(4):23

[100] Ward JA, Evans AJ, Malleson NS. Dynamic calibration of agent-based models using data assimilation. Royal Society Open Science. 2016;**3**(4):150703

[101] Rai S, Hu X. Data assimilation with sensor-informed resampling for building occupancy simulation. In: Proceedings of the 2017 Winter Simulation Conference. Las Vegas, Nevada: IEEE Press; 2017. pp. 1-12

[102] Nguyen HM et al. An alternative approach to avoid overfitting for surrogate models. In: Proceedings of the Winter Simulation Conference. Winter Simulation Conference; 2011

[103] Kashif A et al. Agent based Framework to Simulate Inhabitants' Behaviour in Domestic Settings for Energy Management. In: Proceedings of 3rd International Conference of Agents and Artificial Intelligence. Rome, Italy; 2011. pp. 190-199

[104] Calvez B, Hutzler G. Automatic tuning of agent-based models using genetic algorithms. In: International Workshop on Multi-Agent Systems and Agent-Based Simulation. Springer; 2005

[105] Oloo F, Wallentin G. An adaptive agent-based model of homing pigeons: A genetic algorithm approach. ISPRS International Journal of Geo-Information. 2017;**6**(1):27

[106] Chu X, Buyya R. Service oriented sensor web. In: Sensor networks and Configuration. Berlin, Heidelberg, Germany: Springer; 2007. pp. 51-74

[107] Tan X et al. Agent-as-a-service-based geospatial service aggregation in the cloud: A case study of flood response. Environmental Modelling & Software. 2016;**84**:210-225

[108] Tang W et al. Agent-based modeling within a cyberinfrastructure environment: A service-oriented computing approach. International Journal of Geographical Information Science. 2011;**25**(9):1323-1346

[109] Vinyals M, Rodriguez-Aguilar JA, Cerquides J. A survey on sensor networks from a multiagent perspective. The Computer Journal. 2011;**54**(3): 455-470

[110] Fachada N et al. Parallelization strategies for spatial agent-based models. International Journal of Parallel Programming. 2017;**45**(3):449-481

[111] Parry HR, Bithell M. Large scale agent-based modelling: A review and guidelines for model scaling. In: Agent-based Models of Geographical Systems. Springer; 2012. pp. 271-308

[112] Nichols JA, Hallam TG, Dimitrov DT. Parallel simulation of ecological structured communities: Computational needs, hardware capabilities, and nonlinear applications. Nonlinear Analysis: Theory, Methods & Applications. 2008;**69**(3):832-842

[113] Tang W, Wang S. HPABM: A hierarchical parallel simulation framework for spatially-explicit agent-based models. Transactions in GIS. 2009;**13**(3):315-333

[114] Li Z et al. 4D-SAS: A distributed dynamic-data driven simulation and analysis system for massive spatial agent-based modeling. ISPRS International Journal of Geo-Information. 2016;**5**(4):42

[115] Shook E, Wang S, Tang W. A communication-aware framework for parallel spatially explicit agent-based models. International Journal of Geographical Information Science. 2013;**27**(11):2160-2181

[116] Gong Z et al. Parallel agent-based simulation of individual-level spatial interactions within a multicore computing environment. International Journal of Geographical Information Science. 2013;**27**(6):1152-1170

[117] Pereira GM. Dynamic data driven multi-agent simulation. In Proceedings of the IEEE/WIC/ACM International Conference on Intelligent Agent Technology, IAT 2007. 2008

[118] Xiaoyingjie X, Zhanghao Z, Lisong L. Dynamic data driven multi-agent simulation in maritime traffic. In: Proceedings—2009 International Conference on Computer and Automation Engineering, ICCAE 2009. 2009

[119] Hernandez S et al. From on-body sensors to in-body data for health monitoring and medical robotics: A survey. In: 2014 Global Information Infrastructure and Networking Symposium (GIIS). 2014

[120] Darema F. DDDAS, a key driver for large-scale-big-data and large-scale-big-computing. Procedia Computer Science. 2015;**51**:2463

[121] Van Berkel S et al. Automatic discovery of algorithms for multi-agent systems. In: GECCO'12—Proceedings of the 14th International Conference on Genetic and Evolutionary Computation Companion. 2012

[122] Sottilare RA. Using learner data to influence performance during adaptive tutoring experiences. In: International Conference on Augmented Cognition. Springer; 2014

[123] Shin S et al. Design and analysis of cost-efficient sensor deployment for tracking small UAS with agent-based modeling. Sensors. 2016;**16**(4):575

[124] Yamins D, Nagpal R. Automated global-to-local programming in 1-d spatial multi-agent systems. In: Proceedings of the 7th International

Joint Conference on Autonomous Agents and Multiagent Systems. Vol. 2. International Foundation for Autonomous Agents and Multiagent Systems; 2008

[125] Keller N, Hu X. Data driven simulation modeling for mobile agent-based systems. In: Proceedings of the 2016 Spring Simulation Multiconference—TMS/DEVS Symposium on Theory of Modeling and Simulation, TMS/DEVS 2016. 2016

[126] Grimm V, Railsback SF. Agent-based models in ecology: Patterns and alternative theories of adaptive behaviour. In: Agent-based Computational Modelling. Heidelberg, Germany: Springer; 2006. pp. 139-152

[127] Haghighi M, Cliff D. Sensomax: An agent-based middleware for decentralized dynamic data-gathering in wireless sensor networks. In: 2013 International Conference on Collaboration Technologies and Systems (CTS). 2013

[128] Boulis A, Han C-C, Srivastava MB. Design and implementation of a framework for efficient and programmable sensor networks. In: Proceedings of the 1st International Conference on Mobile Systems, Applications and Services. ACM; 2003

[129] Aiello F et al. Maps: A mobile agent platform for wsns based on java sun spots. Proceedings of ATSM. 2009

[130] Garriga J et al. Expectation-maximization binary clustering for behavioural annotation. PLoS One. 2016;**11**(3):e0151984

[131] Necula E. Analyzing traffic patterns on street segments based on GPS data using R. Transportation Research Procedia. 2015;**10**:276-285

[132] Folino G, Forestiero A, Spezzano G. An adaptive flocking algorithm for performing approximate clustering. Information Sciences. 2009;**179**(18):3059-3078

[133] Jakob M et al. Agents vs. pirates: Multi-agent simulation and optimization to fight maritime piracy. In: 11th International Conference on Autonomous Agents and Multiagent Systems 2012, AAMAS 2012: Innovative Applications Track. 2012

[134] Oremland M, Laubenbacher R. Optimization of agent-based models: Scaling methods and heuristic algorithms. Journal of Artificial Societies and Social Simulation. 2014;**17**(2):6

[135] Heppenstall AJ, Evans AJ, Birkin MH. Genetic algorithm optimisation of an agent-based model for simulating a retail market. Environment and Planning B: Planning and Design. 2007;**34**(6):1051-1070

[136] Zambonelli F et al. Developing pervasive multi-agent systems with nature-inspired coordination. Pervasive and Mobile Computing. 2015;**17**:236-252

[137] Shibuya K. A framework of multi-agent-based modeling, simulation, and computational assistance in an ubiquitous environment. Simulation. 2004;**80**(7-8):367-380

[138] Taillandier P et al. GAMA: A simulation platform that integrates geographical information data, agent-based modeling and multi-scale control. In: International Conference on Principles and Practice of Multi-Agent Systems. Springer; 2010

Chapter 6

Design of the Second-Order Controller by Time-Domain Objective Functions Using Cuckoo Search

Huey-Yang Horng

Abstract

The proportional-integral-derivative (PID) controllers are widely used in many industrial control applications. However, the lead-lag controllers are more practical. Traditionally, time-domain or frequency-domain methods have been used to design a lead-lag controller in order to meet the design specifications. This chapter will focus on the design of controller by optimizing the time-domain objective function. The proposed objective function includes the first peak time, maximum peak time, rise time, maximum overshoot, maximum undershoot, setting time, and steady-state error. In the study, cuckoo search algorithm is adopted to search the optimal controller parameters. Cuckoo search is a recently developed meta-heuristic optimization method, which is a population-based algorithm inspired by the behavior of some cuckoo species in combination with the Lévy flight behavior. A numerical example is simulated to illustrate the use of the proposed method.

Keywords: PID controller, lead-lag controller, controller design, cuckoo search

1. Introduction

In many industrial control applications, proportional-integral-derivative (PID) controllers are probably the most commonly used controllers. Several methods were proposed in the past for tuning the PID controller parameters [1–5]. It is noted the lead-lag controllers provide a more practical alternative. Tan used the Kharitonov and the Hermite-Biehler theorems to compute the parameters of lead-lag controller in [6]. Kuo et al. designed the lead-lag compensator based on vector margin and steady-state error of the step response [7]. Horng used cuckoo search to design lead-lag controllers [8]. It is easy to see that the lead-lag controller is just a special case of the general second-order controllers. Therefore, this paper extends the lead-lag controllers to general second-order controllers. The goal of this paper is to propose a simple second-order controller design procedure using the cuckoo search.

The control design specifications may usually be divided into time-domain and frequency-domain specifications. Time-domain specifications (*TDS*) include the lower and/or upper bounds of the quantities of the time response such as the first peak time, maximum peak time, rise time, maximum overshoot, maximum undershoot, setting time, and steady-state error. Frequency-domain specifications are usually given in terms of the resonant peak, phase margin, resonant frequency, and bandwidth. In this study, we only consider the time-domain specifications.

The main contribution of this study is that we provide a simple controller design procedure for simple second-order controllers. For the problem formulation, some of the time-domain specifications (e.g., desired peak time and maximum overshoot) can be used to fully define a desired simple second-order reference model. With this reference model, we may reasonably specify lower and/or upper bounds for other time-domain specifications. Finally, we define the deviation ratios (i.e., percentage errors) and total deviation ratio. The total deviation ratio, which is the weighted sum of the deviation ratios, will be used as the objective function for the problem. Zero objective value means that all specifications are satisfied. However, there is no guarantee of the zero objective value in the most general cases. Some specifications might actually be violated. The design goal is to choose the best controller parameters so that the objective value is as close to zero as possible.

To search for optimal controller parameters, some optimizer must be employed to solve the aforementioned optimization problem. Since there is usually no analytic formula for the objective function, evolutionary computation algorithms are well suited in this situation to solve this optimization problem. In this study, the meta-heuristic cuckoo search algorithm is adopted to search the optimal controller parameters.

Cuckoo search algorithm is one of the latest meta-heuristic techniques, developed by Yang and Deb [9, 10]. Nowadays, implementations of cuckoo search has proved to be effective in engineering optimization problems [11–13], for example, optimal power system stabilizers [14], load frequency controller design [15], optimal power system [16], synthesis of analog controller [17], etc. Cuckoo search achieved better results than available methods in most cases which appeared in the literature.

The novelty of this study is that the whole controller design problem can be formulated as an optimization problem by considering most important time-domain performance indices as a whole. Moreover, the meta-heuristic cuckoo search algorithm (or any other powerful evolutionary computation algorithms like genetic algorithm or particle swarm optimization) can be adopted to search for the best controller parameters. A numerical example will be provided to illustrate the design process. To show the wide applicability of the proposed method, four different plants and three different time-domain specifications will be used in the illustrative example.

2. Time-domain analysis of control systems

The time response of a control system is typically divided into two parts: the transient response and the steady-state response. The steady-state response is just the part of the total response which remains after the transient has died out. Hence, the steady-state response can still vary in a fixed pattern, such as a ramp function or a parabola function that increases with time.

The underdamped second-order system is a familiar model for physical problems. The detailed understanding of the underdamped response is necessary for both analysis and design. Let us begin by describing the step response for the second-order system. The transfer function of an underdamped second-order system is given by

$$C(s) = \frac{\omega_n^2}{s^2 + 2\xi\omega_n s + \omega_n^2}, \quad 0 < \xi < 1. \tag{1}$$

A typical unit-step response is shown in **Figure 1**. In this figure, y_{ss}, y_M, and y_m denote the steady-state value, maximum response value, and the response value where the maximum undershoot occurs, respectively. Moreover, T_r, T_p, and T_s are the rise time, peak time, and settling time, respectively.

We now describe seven time-domain specifications (TDS) used in objective function in more detail:

1. Rise time T_r. It is the time required for the step response to rise from 10 to 90% of its final value.

2. First peak time T_f. It is the time to reach the first peak.

3. Maximum peak time T_p. It is the time to reach the maximum peak.

4. Maximum overshoot MOS. This is defined as

$$MOS = \begin{cases} \dfrac{y_M - y_{ss}}{y_{ss}}, & \text{if } y_M > y_{ss}, \\ 0, & \text{if } y_M \le y_{ss}. \end{cases} \tag{2}$$

5. Maximum undershoot MUS. It is defined as

$$y_m = \min(y(t)), \quad t \ge T_f,$$
$$MUS = \begin{cases} \dfrac{y_{ss} - y_m}{y_{ss}}, & \text{if } y_m < y_{ss}, \\ 0, & \text{if } y_m \ge y_{ss}. \end{cases} \tag{3}$$

6. Settling time T_s. This is the time required for the step response to decrease and stay within a specified ±2% of the final value.

7. Steady state error E_{ss}. It is the difference between the desired and actual responses.

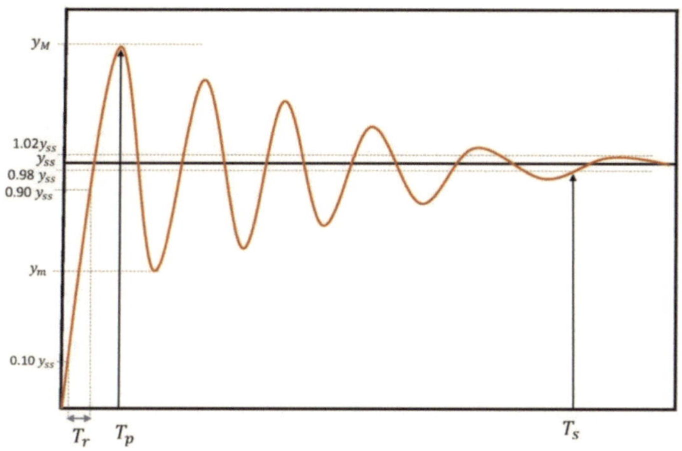

Figure 1.
Unit-step response for underdamped second-order systems.

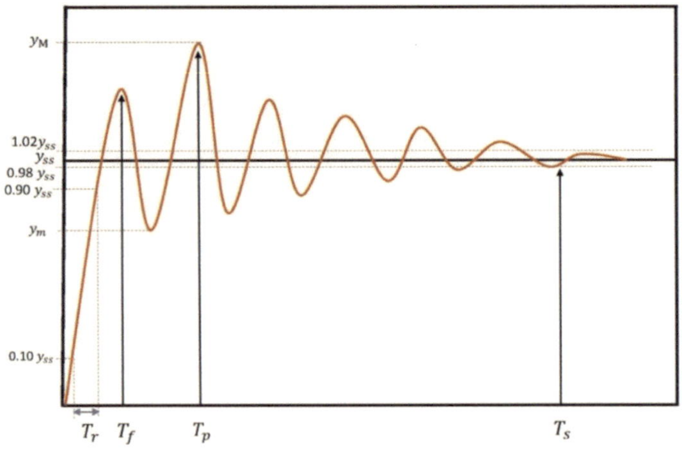

Figure 2.
Unit-step response for some underdamped higher-order systems.

Notice that for second-order systems, the first peak time is always the maximum peak time. However, for underdamped higher-order systems, they may not be the same, as illustrated in **Figure 2**. In general, the response of an underdamped high-order system is similar to that of an underdamped second-order system.

Notice also that the following relationships hold for second-order systems, which will be used in the illustrative example:

$$\xi = \frac{|\ln(MOS)|}{\sqrt{\pi^2 + \ln^2(MOS)}} \tag{4}$$

$$\omega_n = \frac{\pi}{T_p\sqrt{1-\xi^2}} \tag{5}$$

In the design process, a second-order system with satisfactory performances is designated as the reference standard. All the desired specifications with lower and upper bounds are tabulated. Note that the lower bounds of maximum overshot, maximum undershot, setting time, and steady error are set to zero.

3. Proposed controller

The transfer function of general second-order controller is written as

$$G_c(s) = K\left(\frac{cs^2 + ds + 1}{as^2 + bs + 1}\right), \tag{6}$$

where $K > 0$, a, b, $c, d \in \Re$. It is easy to see that the phase lead-lag controller is just a special case of general second-order controller. The overall control system in this study is shown in **Figure 3**, where $G_p(s)$ is the transfer function of the plant. Besides, $r(t)$, $y(t)$, and $e(t)$ denote the reference input, output, and error signal.

For the feedback control system shown in **Figure 3**, the overall response is determined by the parameters of the controller. To establish the proposed time-domain objective function, we first define a function called the deviation ratio (DR), where TDS stands for the time-domain specifications described in Section 2:

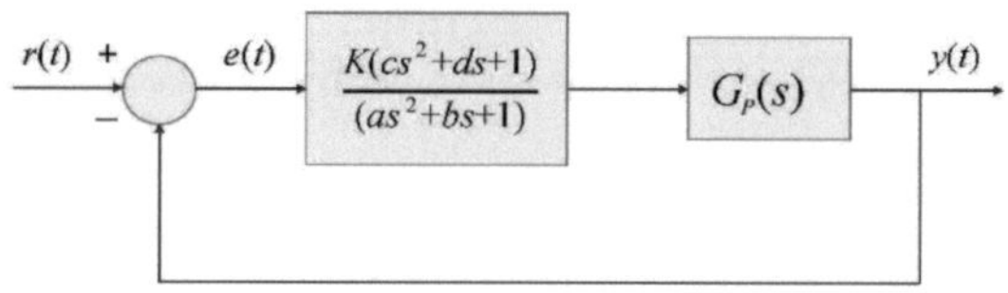

Figure 3.
Unity feedback system with second-order controller.

$$DR(TDS(K,a,b,c,d)) = \begin{cases} \dfrac{TDS(K,a,b,c,d) - TDS\_ub}{TDS\_ub}, & \text{if } TDS(K,a,b,c,d) > TDS\_ub, \\ \dfrac{TDS\_lb - TDS(K,a,b,c,d)}{TDS\_lb}, & \text{if } TDS(K,a,b,c,d) < TDS\_lb, \\ 0, & \text{otherwise,} \end{cases} \quad (7)$$

where $TDS(K,a,b,c,d)$ is any one of the time-domain specifications defined in the last section. In practical designs, some tolerances in time-domain specifications are allowed. Therefore, each of the time-domain specifications has a corresponding lower limit (TDS_lb) and an upper bound (TDS_ub). $DR(TDS(K,a,b,c,d))$ is a measure of how the actual quantity is close to the desired interval specified by lower limit and upper limit. For example, if the value of $DR(T_r(K,a,b,c,d))$ is zero, where the relevant quantity is the rise time, then this means that the rise time lies in the desired interval. That is, the specification is fully satisfied.

Next, we define the objective function $TDR(K,a,b,c,d)$, called the total deviation ratio (TDR), used in this study as follows:

$$\begin{aligned} TDR(K,a,b,c,d) = [&w_1 \cdot (DR(T_r(K,a,b,c,d)))^2 + w_2 \cdot \left(DR\left(T_f(K,a,b,c,d)\right)\right)^2 \\ &+w_3 \cdot \left(DR\left(T_p(K,a,b,c,d)\right)\right)^2 \\ &+w_4 \cdot (DR(MOS(K,a,b,c,d)))^2 + w_5 \cdot (DR(MUS(K,a,b,c,d)))^2 \\ &+w_6 \cdot (DR(T_s(K,a,b,c,d)))^2 + w_7 \cdot (DR(E_{ss}(K,a,b,c,d)))^2] / \sum_{i=1}^{7} w_i \end{aligned} \quad (8)$$

In Eq. (8), ω_i, $i = 1, 2, \cdots, 7$ represents weights that reflect the relative importance of the corresponding terms.

Eqs. (6)–(8) are improved versions of those in Ref. [8]. Once we defined the deviation ratio and total deviation ratio, the problem of the design controller becomes the minimization of $TDR(K,a,b,c,d)$ for all possible parameters. Now, we can use various optimization methods to implement the controller design. In the paper, the cuckoo search algorithm is used to minimize the objective function. Further, if the $TDR(K,a,b,c,d)$ is zero, all specifications are within the range of the design specifications.

4. Cuckoo search algorithm

In this section, the cuckoo search algorithm is briefly introduced. This algorithm was proposed by Yang and Deb in [9, 10]. Cuckoo search represents an optimized meta-heuristic algorithm that is biologically inspired by the way cuckoo looks for a nest where they could lay eggs in combination with the Lévy flight behavior of some birds and fruit flies.

Now we briefly describe some breeding behaviors of cuckoos. As pointed out in [9], some cuckoo species often lay the eggs in the nests of other host birds, especially those that just spawned eggs. Some host birds can engage direct conflict with the intruding cuckoos. If a host bird discovers the eggs are not their own, they may either throw these alien eggs away or simply abandon its nest and build a new nest elsewhere [9]. Some cuckoo species are often very specialized in the mimicry in color and pattern of the eggs of a few chosen host species, which reduces the probability of their eggs being abandoned and thus increases their reproductively.

In the optimization algorithm, each nest represents a potential solution. The process of cuckoo search algorithm is simplified by three rules [10]:

1. Each cuckoo lays an egg in a randomly selected nest.

2. The best nests will carry over to the next generation.

3. The number of available host nest is fixed, and there is a positive probability that the egg laid by a cuckoo is discovered by the host bird.

There are many variants of the cuckoo search algorithms. In the following, we describe a commonly used version. This algorithm uses a combination of a local random walk and the global random walk, controlled by a switching parameter p_a. This allows for proper balance between exploration and exploitation of the solution space. The local and global random walks for generating the new solution of for cuckoo i can be written as, respectively,

$$x_i^{t+1} = x_i^t + \alpha s \otimes H(p_a - \varepsilon) \otimes \left(x_j^t - x_k^t\right) \tag{9}$$

$$x_i^{t+1} = x_i^t + \alpha L(s, \lambda) \tag{10}$$

$$L(s, \lambda) = \frac{\lambda \Gamma(\lambda) \sin(\pi\lambda/2)}{\pi} \cdot \frac{1}{s^{1+\lambda}}, \quad s \geq s_0 \geq 0 \tag{11}$$

In Eqs. (9)–(11), the notations are explained as follows:

x_i^{t+1}	next position of cuckoo i
x_i^t	current position of cuckoo i
α	step size scaling factor
s	step size
$\otimes$	entry-wise multiplication of two vectors
H	Heaviside function
p_a	switching parameter used to switch local and global walks
ε	a random number drawn from a uniform distribution
x_j^t, x_k^t	current positions of cuckoos j and k selected by random permutation
$L(s, \lambda)$	Lévy distribution used to define the step size of random walk

5. Design procedure

In the design procedure, a second-order system with satisfactory performances is designated as the reference standard. All of the seven desired specifications with lower bounds and upper bounds are tabulated. After that, we set solution vector as

(K, a, b, c, d) and use cuckoo search algorithm to find the minimum value of $TDR(K, a, b, c, d)$ in Eq. (8). To save computation time, the initial populations of 25 host nests are selected using Routh-Hurwitz criterion (for linear time-invariant plants) so that the closed-loop systems are stable.

In the following design procedure, we set maximum generation to be 1000 and $p_a = 0.25$. The optimization process is hierarchical. First, run cuckoo search 25 times to get minimum values. Then the 25 minimum values become elite group. Next, run cuckoo search one more time, and use the group as initial host nests. The final result is the parameters for the second-order controller.

6. Illustrative example

In the section, a numerical example is provided to illustrate the design procedure. In the following simulations, four different plants are used for comparison, which are described in **Table 1**.

As an instance, the step response of the uncompensated system of Plant 1 is shown in **Figure 4**. The peak time is estimated to be 2.4 s, the maximum overshoot is 26.5398%, and the steady-state error E_{ss} is 0.5. Assume we are not satisfied with these time-domain performance indices. Consequently, compensation must be designed for better performances.

Experiment 1. Keep in mind that our reference model is a simple second-order system defined in Eq. (1). Assume that the desired peak time T_p is set to be 1 s and the maximum tolerable overshoot is 0.03. Now we can use Eqs. (4) and (5) to calculate the corresponding damping ratio ξ and natural frequency ω_n, respectively. This determines the desired reference model in Eq. (1). Based on the resulting reference model, we can calculate its seven performance indices depicted in Section 2 in order to establish reasonable bounds for these performance indices. We may put 2% tolerance on rise time T_r, first peak time T_f, and maximum peak time T_p. Only upper bounds are specified for the remaining four performance indices. The full specifications for Experiment 1 are listed in the second column of **Table 2**.

We set all the weights to be 1, i.e., $\omega_i = 1, i = 1, 2, \ldots, 7$. Suppose the maximum steady-state error is limited to $[0.001, 0.022]$, and then we can set the range of K to $[7.4091, 166.5000]$; the ranges of a, b, c, and d are all set to $[-100, 100]$. The specified ranges of controller parameters are listed in **Table 3**.

The resulting control parameters are shown in **Table 4**.

The time-domain performances of the resulting closed-loop systems are shown in **Table 5**. Notice that the final objective values for four plants shown in the final row of **Table 5** are all zeros, which means that all seven design specifications are all met using our controller design methods.

The time responses due to unit-step input of the resulting four closed-loop systems are shown in **Figure 5**. These responses look quite nice.

	Transfer function	System type	Closed-loop stability
Plant 1	$G_p(s) = \frac{120}{s^2+12s+20}$	0	Stable
Plant 2	$G_p(s) = \frac{100s+1}{s(10s+1)(s+1)}$	1	Stable
Plant 3	$G_p(s) = \frac{100}{(s+1)(s+2)(s+4)}$	0	Unstable
Plant 4	$G_p(s) = \frac{1}{s(s+1)}$	1	Stable

Table 1.
Description of the four plants.

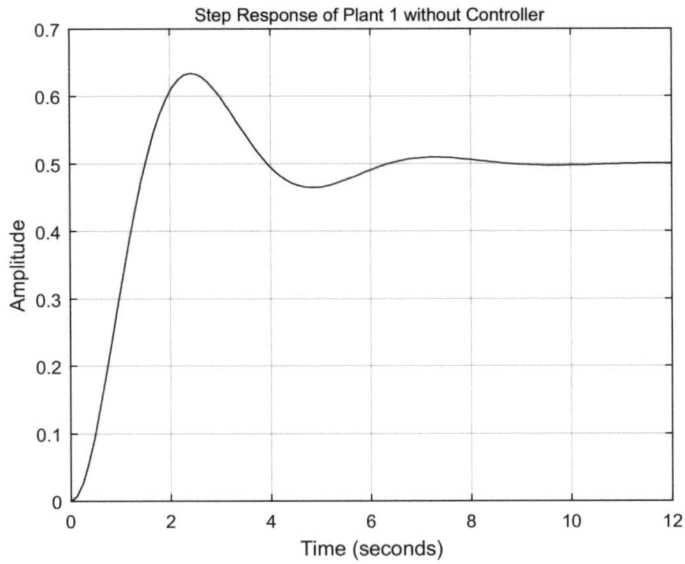

Figure 4.
Step response of the Plant 1 without controller.

	Experiment 1	Experiment 2	Experiment 3
T_r	[0.4730, 0.4923]	[0.7095, 0.7385]	[0.9461, 0.9847]
T_f	[0.9788, 1.0188]	[1.4682, 1.5281]	[1.9576, 2.0375]
T_p	[0.9788, 1.0188]	[1.4682, 1.5281]	[1.9576, 2.0375]
MOS	≤ 0.03	≤ 0.03	≤ 0.03
MUS	≤ 0.02	≤ 0.02	≤ 0.02
T_s	≤ 1.0724	≤ 1.6086	≤ 2.1448
E_{ss}	≤ 0.02	≤ 0.02	≤ 0.02

Table 2.
Design specifications.

	Plant 1	Plant 2	Plant 3	Plant 4
K	[7.4091,166.5000]	[45.4545, 1000]	[7.4091, 166.5000]	[45.4545, 1000]
a	[−100,100]	[−100,100]	[−100,100]	[−100,100]
b	[−100,100]	[−100,100]	[−100,100]	[−100,100]
c	[−100,100]	[−100,100]	[−100,100]	[−100,100]
d	[−100,100]	[−100,100]	[−100,100]	[−100,100]

Table 3.
Search ranges of controller parameters.

Experiment 2. In this experiment, assume that the first peak time and the maximum peak time are both set to 1.5 s. Following the procedure in Experiment 1, the full design specifications for Experiment 2 are also listed in **Table 2**. The specified ranges of controller parameters are listed in **Table 3**. The resulting control parameters are shown in **Table 6**.

	Plant 1	Plant 2	Plant 3	Plant 4
K	8.4963	995.7351	14.6760	934.2808
a	100.0000	1.6668	1.7609	−0.1364
b	30.4229	8.8714	60.2882	−0.8138
c	3.1336	98.4428	0.6624	−86.8253
d	7.3230	48.7921	1.2683	−85.5579

Table 4.
Resulting controller parameters in Experiment 1.

	Plant 1	Plant 2	Plant 3	Plant 4
T_r	0.4804	0.4734	0.4923	0.4735
T_f	1.0131	1.0131	0.9804	1.0131
T_p	1.0131	1.0131	0.9804	1.0131
MOS	0.0000	0.0294	0.0297	0.0281
MUS	0.0179	0.0004	0.0093	0.0004
T_s	0.7717	1.0295	0.9968	1.0295
E_{ss}	0.0192	0.0010	0.0054	0.0011
TDR	0	0	0	0

Table 5.
Time-domain performance indices of the resulting systems in Experiment 1.

The time-domain performances of the resulting closed-loop systems are shown in **Table 7**. Notice again that the final objective values for four plants are all zeros, which means that all seven design specifications are all met using our controller design methods.

The time responses due to unit-step input of the resulting four closed-loop systems are shown in **Figure 6**.

Experiment 3. In this experiment, assume that the first peak time and the maximum peak time are both set to 2.0 s. Following the procedure in Experiment 1, the full design specifications for Experiment 3 are also shown in **Table 2**. The specified ranges of controller parameters are listed in **Table 3**. The resulting control parameters are shown in **Table 8**.

The time-domain performances of the resulting closed-loop systems are shown in **Table 9**. Notice that the final objective values for four plants are zeros, which means that all seven design specifications are met using our controller design methods.

The time responses due to unit-step input of the resulting four closed-loop systems are shown in **Figure 7**.

In the illustrative example above, four different plants and three different time-domain specifications were used. As illustrated in the preceding example, before searching the best controller parameters, we first use some of the time-domain specifications (e.g., desired peak time and maximum overshoot) to fully specify the desired simple second-order reference model. Then we may use this reference model to define reasonable bounds for other time-domain specifications. Finally, we define the deviation ratios (i.e., percentage errors) and total deviation ratio as the objective function. If the final value of the objective function is zero, then all seven specifications are satisfied. But, in the most general cases, there is no

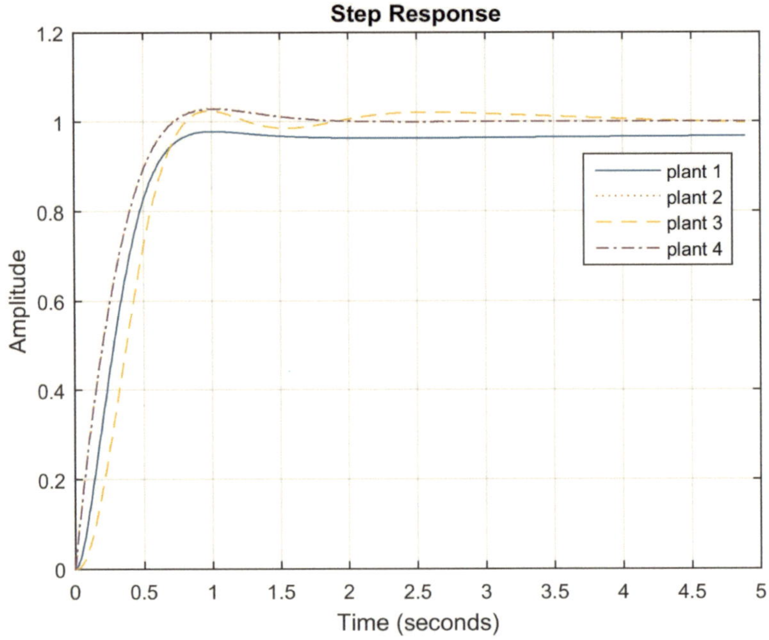

Figure 5.
Step responses of four resulting systems in Experiment 1.

	Plant 1	Plant 2	Plant 3	Plant 4
K	8.4963	995.7351	14.6760	934.2808
a	100.0000	1.6668	1.7609	−0.1364
b	30.4229	8.8714	60.2882	−0.8138
c	3.1336	98.4428	0.6624	−86.8253
d	7.3230	48.7921	1.2683	−85.5579

Table 6.
Resulting controller parameters in Experiment 2.

	Plant 1	Plant 2	Plant 3	Plant 4
T_r	0.7133	0.7105	0.7384	0.7102
T_f	1.5197	1.5197	1.4952	1.5197
T_p	1.5197	1.5197	1.4952	1.5197
MOS	0.0103	0.0282	0.0299	0.0281
MUS	0.0128	0.0004	0.0139	0.0004
T_s	1.0929	1.5442	1.5197	1.5442
E_{ss}	0.0198	0.0010	0.0129	0.0010
TDR	0	0	0	0

Table 7.
Time-domain performance indices of the resulting systems in Experiment 2.

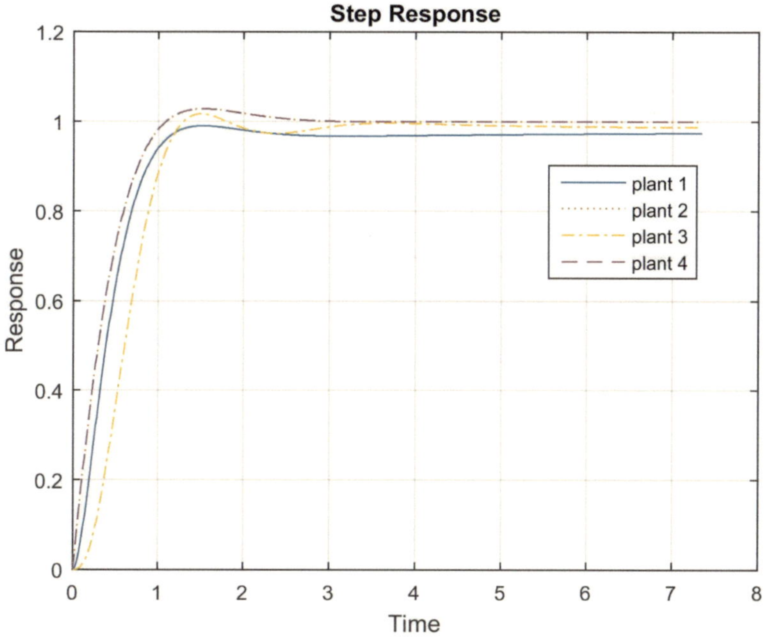

Figure 6.
Step responses of four resulting systems in Experiment 2.

	Plant 1	Plant 2	Plant 3	Plant 4
K	8.4963	995.7351	14.6760	934.2808
a	100.0000	1.6668	1.7609	−0.1364
b	30.4229	8.8714	60.2882	−0.8138
c	3.1336	98.4428	0.6624	−86.8253
d	7.3230	48.7921	1.2683	−85.5579

Table 8.
Resulting controller parameters in Experiment 3.

	Plant 1	Plant 2	Plant 3	Plant 4
T_r	0.9656	0.9468	0.9794	0.9467
T_f	1.9935	2.0262	1.9609	2.0262
T_p	1.9935	2.0262	1.9609	2.0262
MOS	0.0024	0.0292	0.0220	0.0284
MUS	0.0154	0.0004	0.0138	0.0004
T_s	1.4927	2.0589	1.9935	2.0589
E_{ss}	0.0198	0.0010	0.0199	0.0011
TDR	0	0	0	0

Table 9.
Time-domain performance indices of the resulting systems in Experiment 3.

guarantee that the final value of the objective function will always be zero. In that case, some specifications might be violated. The design goal is to choose the best controller parameters so that the objective value is as close to zero as possible. In the

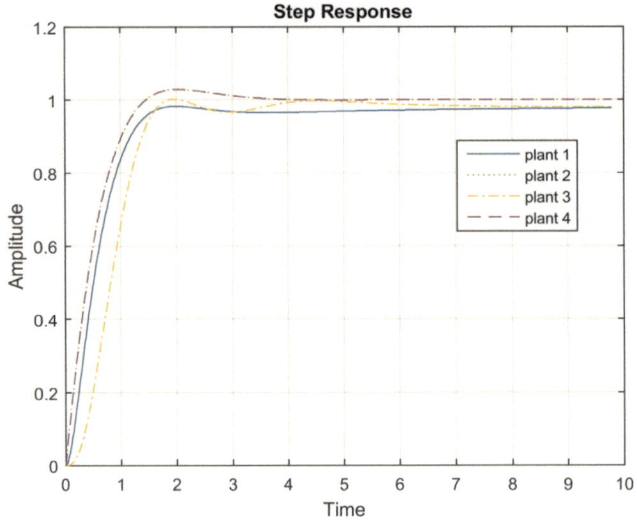

Figure 7.
Step responses of four resulting systems in Experiment 3.

simulations above, it is fortunate that the final objective values of all simulations are zeros and all seven time-domain specifications are met. This also shows that the cuckoo search is an excellent optimizer for searching best controller parameters.

7. Conclusion

In this study, a design procedure of second-order controller for various plants has been proposed. The final controller was obtained by minimizing a time-domain cost function which is weighted sum of important time-domain performance indices including the rise time, first peak time, maximum peak time, maximum overshoot, maximum undershoot, setting time, and steady-state error. In our approach, the desired design specifications were built via a good second-order reference model. Cuckoo search algorithm was adopted to search the optimal controller parameters. Detailed simulations with different design specifications for four plants were provided to illustrate the use of the proposed design method. From the simulation results, the resulting performances of the closed-loop systems are quite good by using the proposed method, which justifies the usefulness of our method. We wish to point out that the methodology proposed in this study can easily be modified to handle the time delay or nonlinear plants. This constitutes an interesting future research topic.

Author details

Huey-Yang Horng
Department of Electronic Engineering, I-Shou University, Kaohsiung City, Taiwan, R.O.C

*Address all correspondence to: hyhorng@isu.edu.tw

References

[1] Panda S, Sahu BK, Mohanty PK. Design and performance analysis of PID controller for an automatic voltage regulator system using simplified particle swarm optimization. Journal of the Franklin Institute. 2012;**349**(8): 2609-2625

[2] Perng JW, Chen GY, Hsieh SC. Optimal PID controller design based on PSO-RBFNN for wind turbine systems. Energies. 2014;**7**(1):191-209

[3] Kesarkar AA, Selvaganesan N. Tuning of optimal fractional-order PID controller using an artificial bee colony algorithm. Systems Science & Control Engineering. 2015;**3**:99-105

[4] Ghosal S, Darbar R, Neogi B, Das A, Tibarewala DN. Application of swarm intelligence computation techniques in PID controller tuning: A review. In: Proceedings of the InConINDIA 2012, AISC 132; 2012. pp. 195-208

[5] Saroja K, Stefka Sharon R, Meena S, Chitra K. Multi-loop PID controller design for distillation column using firefly algorithm. International Journal of Engineering and Technology (IJET). 2017;**9**(2):1404-1410

[6] Tan N. Computation of stabilizing lag/lead controller parameters. Computers and Electrical Engineering. 2003;**29**:835-849

[7] Kuo YS, Lin JY, Tang JC, Hsieh JG. Lead-lag compensator design based on vector margin and steady-state error of the step response via particle swarm optimization. In: International Conference on Fuzzy Theory and Its Applications (iFuzzy); 2016. pp. 96-101

[8] Horng HY. Design of lead-lag controller via time-domain objective function by using cuckoo search. In: Lecture Notes in Electrical Engineering (ICITES2013); Vol. 293; 2014. pp. 1083-1091

[9] Yang XS, Deb S. Cuckoo search via Lévy flights. In: World Congress on Nature & Biologically Inspired Computing, December 2009; India. USA: IEEE Publications; 2009. pp. 210-214

[10] Yang XS, Deb S. Engineering optimisation by cuckoo search. International Journal of Mathematical Modelling and Numerical Optimisation. 2010;**1**(4):330-343

[11] Fister I Jr, Fister D, Fister I. Comprehensive review of cuckoo search variants and hybrids. International Journal of Mathematical Modelling and Numerical Optimisation. 2013;**4**(4): 387-409

[12] Yang XS, Deb S. Cuckoo search: Recent advances and applications. Neural Computing and Applications. 2014;**24**(1):169-174

[13] Shehab M, Khader AT, Al-Betar MA. A survey on applications and variants of the cuckoo search algorithm. Applied Soft Computing. 2017;**61**: 1041-1059

[14] Abd Elazim SM, Ali ES. Optimal power system stabilizers design via cuckoo search algorithm. International Journal of Electrical Power & Energy Systems. 2016;**75**:99-107

[15] Abdelaziz AY, Ali ES. Load frequency controller design via artificial cuckoo search algorithm. Electric Power Components & Systems. 2016;**44**(1): 90-98

[16] Anh L, Tam NM, Nghia LT, Anh QH. Optimal power system stabilizer parameters tuned by cuckoo search algorithm. International Journal

of Engineering Research & Technology (IJERT). 2017;**6**(11):24-28

[17] Wongkaew B, Puangdownreong D. Application of cuckoo search to synthesize analog controllersi. nternational journal of circuits Systems and Signal Processing. 2019;**13**:79-84